# BECOMING WHOLE
## A MEMOIR

## MINDY TSAI

Published by Etcetera Books
Brookline, MA 02445

ISBN: 978-0-578-51031-6 (paperback)
ISBN: 978-0-578-51032-3 (ebook)
LCCN: 2019905682

*For my friends*
*who did not leave me alone*

# AUTHOR'S NOTE

At age thirty, right around my birthday, something significant happened, and I didn't really understand what it was: I became a schizophrenic.

I can't show you physically what I have. It is impossible to prove that I have a brain disease using any scientific test based on current medicine and technology. The diagnosis was and could only be based on what I told the doctors about my behaviors and experiences. I never felt there was anything wrong with me or my brain. I never saw a big cut with blood gushing out, nor did I have a deadly headache that affected how I lived my life.

What I can do is to tell you a story. With a humble heart, I want to tell you about what I experienced from my perspective, with vivid description and my most complete memory. I have thought about this part of my life over and over again during the last decade, looking for logical patterns to make sense of it all. With every reflection and every new experience with schizophrenia, I see my brain and myself more clearly.

This is a personal story from the nonclinical perspective of an independent and educated adult woman with schizophrenia. I hope by sharing this, I can give you a sense of what schizophrenia has been like for me, so we can all better understand this incredible brain disease.

# CONTENTS

Prologue                                    1

**PART 1: JOE**                             7

1.  A WHOLE NEW WORLD                        9
2.  A RUNAWAY MIND                          16
3.  ·A BREAKDOWN                            24

**PART 2: ME**                             31

4.  MY BEGINNINGS                           33
5.  STEPS FORWARD, STEPS BACK               49
6.  SECOND CHANCE                           72
7.  LOCKED UP                               97

**PART 3: ME, LATER**                     141

8.  LEARNING AND SHARING                   143
9.  STILL HARD, RELAPSES                   156
10. DATING                                 161
11. A NEW BEGINNING                        167

Conclusion                                 174
Acknowledgments                            175

# PROLOGUE

On a sunny day, as I was getting ready to go to work, I heard my first voice clearly. Later on, I affectionately called him Joe. It was not like dreaming or having thoughts in my mind. To me, it was having a conversation with a real person whom I couldn't see. Exactly that. No different. He sounded gentle and kind. He even made me smile.

Joe entered my life when I was truly alone at age thirty. I had just broken up with my boyfriend. I'd gotten laid off from my first job and started a new job. While trying to live on my own again after the breakup, my apartment was broken into. Worried for my own safety, I moved into a house with housemates. I was emotionally isolated, but I didn't know or analyze the situation I was in. For the first time in my life, I was determined to become a stronger person, living my life with only books, music, gym, and work, and did not reach out to any of my friends.

Joe noticed me. In my mind, Joe was a young man my age who hid himself from me, but was always close by. I felt a strong presence through his voice and what I thought he did, but I never saw him in person. Joe started playing music for me by calling into different local radio stations and making song requests. When I turned on the radio, he'd have something ready for me. He loved the challenge of picking music I loved. He was able to tell I loved a song because I'd start singing along and smiling. Sometimes he surprised me with a song at home, at work, or at the grocery store. I felt he could read my mind by the way he responded to my feelings and thoughts through music.

Joe didn't want to leave me alone even though I stuck to my routine every day. He started making life fun for me with elaborate hide-and-seek games in the city. When I explored and wandered around Boston, he'd guess where I was headed. I often didn't have a destination in mind. He played right into my spontaneity. He left clues for me to figure out. One time I was on the T, and he convinced everyone to get off at a certain stop. When I saw the whole train emptied out, I thought, *Where is everyone going? Should I follow and check it out too?* I didn't want to miss out.

No one had ever stopped me on the street until after Joe entered my life. I thought he might've sent his friends to interrupt me while I wandered the city. A guy showed me a map, asking for directions. Another person stopped me to take a picture of him and his friends. Another man even asked me to take a picture with him. I wondered why, all of a sudden, everyone was interested in talking to me.

At first Joe brought beautiful feelings to my life. One night, I was wandering on my own at Faneuil Hall. Under the dark night sky, there was a young man standing at a corner, a street performer. He was alone. I was alone. We saw each other, and he started playing his guitar and singing. He had a great voice. It was soft and sweet. After the song ended, I turned around to leave. Someone in the dark from another corner said, "Don't go. Talk to him." I was startled. I turned to where the voice was coming from and saw an older man. I didn't realize there was another person there. I felt embarrassed by my own presence, that I had been discovered. I quickly ran away, back to the T, back home, but I had a big smile on my face because I'd loved the acoustic music. *Isn't it so lucky I ran into the singer all by myself even though it was interrupted by another stranger? Had Joe sent him?*

Joe was with me at the movie theaters and gym. His friends were kicking my seat, coughing, laughing, trying to send me hints. *What are they trying to tell me?* I froze in my seat, slightly confused and startled. I couldn't focus on the movie. Even though it seemed like something meaningful was being conveyed, I couldn't figure out what it was. I had no guesses, either. In my mind, I just ended up with a bunch of disconnected observations. I would continue to puzzle over them for weeks!

After a frustrating day at work, I went to the gym to run off some steam. In the running room, all the treadmills were being used except one, left just for me. So lucky! I was moved and encouraged by this room of strangers, all women, running. I almost cried, feeling the strong and positive energy in the room, especially after having a difficult day at work. How amazing that they were all there with me, for me, because I needed the support. *Is this possible? Are they all friends of Joe's?*

I started getting curious about Joe. I wanted to meet him. I wanted to make him show up. One night, after he played several songs for me on the radio, I told him, "Let's meet tonight!" I put on my jacket and went out. I listened to honking and other signals he gave me and ended up near Fenway Park. I waited and waited under the stars. It was past midnight, but I didn't care. Joe didn't show. On the walk home, I heard Joe say, "Go home." That was the only thing he said to me that day.

Another night, I told him I wanted to go ice skating. I loved skating. "I'll wait for you in the lobby," I told him. I waited for him for about thirty minutes. No one showed up. I decided to go on my own anyway. Why spoil the good mood? I went to Frog Pond, rented a pair of white skates, and skated around the pond. A group of guys showed up and cheered loudly. They had signs, but I couldn't make out what they were. They shouted, but I couldn't hear clearly what they said. I was startled again. *Why are they with me at the skating pond? What are they trying to say? Did Joe send them?* This time, Joe did not speak to me at all.

As time went on, Joe seemed to be around even more, and he was able to do more. While I worked, he could see me and my laptop. While I was typing, he corrected my mistakes by moving my mouse to show me what he meant. Sometimes, when I was really focused on an email, he would interrupt me by typing an extra letter to distract me. I thought he wanted to let me know he was there with me.

One weekend morning, I woke up thinking about Joe. I might've dreamed about him. It was fuzzy. While in bed, I closed my eyes and started chanting: "Please let him be a real person. Please let him be a real person. Please let him be a real person." I continued for about five minutes. I really, really wanted to meet him in person. I wanted to ask him about all he might be doing for me: playing music for me, going to places with me, sending me messages.

I believed he got in touch with my friends because I started to hear the voices of my friends in addition to Joe's. They had parties while I was in my living room. A friend asked me to call her because she hadn't heard from me in a while: "Call me! You have to call me!" "Let's play a word game! Complete the sentence for me," a different friend said. "Let's listen to music." They took turns spending time with me. I didn't understand why my friends were getting in touch with me this way, through Joe, but I was happy to hear from them.

I took a vacation in Taipei. During the two-week trip, I thought of Joe twice. One day I woke up and heard birds talking outside. I thought, *Is that him trying to get my attention?* I didn't think I would feel Joe's presence when I was so far away from home. I almost cried. I didn't want to think about him while visiting my relatives. I felt confused and interrupted.

As our relationship continued, Joe became less amazing. Sometimes he was even abusive. No matter what I asked him, I wouldn't get a response. He just ignored my questions. At the same time, he wouldn't stop talking to me either. He could talk to me any time he wanted. The talking just kept on coming. I couldn't turn it off. I couldn't sleep; I couldn't focus at work. I tried different ways to talk sense into Joe. *I am not anyone important*, I said in my head. *Tell me what you want! Are you not bored watching me all this time?* I tried to listen very carefully to see what he really wanted. I tried to ignore him, hoping he would go away. Eventually, I stopped living my life and ended up reacting to Joe's world as many voices talked, talked, and talked.

Eventually, I was locked up because of Joe.

— Part 1 —

# JOE

# 1

# A WHOLE NEW WORLD

Fall and Winter 2002

## MY FIRST VOICE

I woke up in my bedroom and was getting dressed. All of a sudden, I heard a young man talking. Maybe the talking was from the wall, from next door. I looked at the white wall. I thought, *Let me walk outside the house to see if I can still hear him.* I stepped out the front door, and there was silence for about five seconds. Then, the voice said, clearly, "Can you hear me?"

I stood in front of the door and locked it, ready for work. I had been a project manager and software consultant since I'd graduated from college. I enjoyed what I did, working with smart teams of analysts and engineers, solving interesting business problems by leveraging technology. On this particular day, I did what I always did: I walked to my office in a red brick building in East Cambridge. I lived on a quiet residential street in the same neighborhood. Two-floor houses lined both sides of the street all the way from home to work. Working-class cars were parked one after another. A few scattered trees dotted the sidewalks. This was not a popular area. If you didn't live here, there was no reason to come here. I could see no one near me.

"Yes," I said quietly and smiled.

"Don't smile. You're going to look silly if you walk down the street, talking to yourself and smiling on your own."

*Okay,* I thought in response.

"You need to ask someone for help," the voice said.

*Jennifer?* I thought immediately.

"No, it has to be a single guy."

I thought to myself, *Is this some sort of joke?*

"No, this is not a joke. This is serious," the voice said.

I didn't think it was odd that the voice belonged to a young man. What I wondered was how someone was able to talk to me this way. I tried to think about it logically. As I walked into my building and down the hallway toward my office, I looked around for the source of the sound. Was he using some high-tech equipment I didn't know about? I looked in the corners of the hallway. Were there speakers around me I couldn't see? All I saw were red bricks on the wall and gray carpets on the floor. I looked up to the windows. Was this voice coming from a satellite? All I saw was the bright blue sky. Distracted by my own thoughts, Joe disappeared, and our first conversation ended as I reached my cubicle.

I thought about what the voice and I had just talked about. *Okay, a single guy.* I decided to get help from Dan, another employee. I had a crush on him, but we didn't really know each other. I made up my mind and didn't hesitate. I marched to where I knew Dan would be. I didn't notice if anyone else was around. I tapped Dan on the back of his shoulder, and he turned around and faced me. "Can I talk to you for a second? Can you come with me?" I said in front of his cubicle. He didn't say anything or act surprised. He just got up from his seat and followed me.

Dan and I walked out of the office and were standing in front of the building on the sidewalk. We stood quietly facing each other next to a brick wall at the entrance to the office. I avoided eye contact and looked down at the ground. Dan seemed to be amused. I didn't know what to say to him. I opened my mouth, closed it, and opened it again as I rubbed my hands against each other. I was suddenly confused. I remembered I was told to ask for help. But for what? I tried to open my mouth again. He waited. No words came out. My face and ears felt hot. I gave up and apologized, "Never mind. Sorry."

"Okay, I'm going to get coffee," he said politely, gave a gentle smile, and walked away, toward the mall. He didn't seem annoyed or alerted. I watched him go. I stood on the sidewalk alone. I was still confused. *Okay. What was that?* I asked myself. I didn't think it through before dragging Dan out of the office. I must have made a horrible impression. I was frustrated and said to myself, *Don't ever listen to him (Joe) or do what he says. That was stupid.* I dismissed the whole thing as an annoyance and went back to work. I never discussed the incident with Dan or anyone.

## MY NEW LANGUAGE

Joe started speaking to me more and more. He spoke to me when I was alone in my room. He only showed up when I was alone. His voice continued to be soft, calm, and gentle. He never yelled at me or talked over me. With the exception of our first interaction, I never "talked' to Joe using my mouth. I spoke words to him in my head silently. Anyone else around would have seen me as being quiet, as not having a conversation with anyone. But I was having conversations with Joe continuously. My mind focused completely on his voice when he talked. My eyes took a slight backseat to my ears as I tried to continue to go about doing things while Joe commented on what I was doing. He always enunciated his words. I had no trouble understanding him. When I turned on the radio on my bookshelf, he said, "Good!" When I opened a book to start reading, he said, "Let's think about this." During the weekends, the talking would go on the whole time I was alone in my room. Sometimes I told him what I thought of him. In my head, I told him he had a crappy job because he had to babysit me. I said, it seemed to me he didn't have time to eat or sleep. When Joe was not around, I thought, *Why would someone go through this effort to talk to me this way and not just talk to me face-to-face?* I felt that I was nobody special. Whichever way these conversations were taking place, must be a rather expensive and massive effort. Joe didn't give me any answers. He just continued to hang out with me from time to time.

At some point, Joe said to me, "One honk means right. Two honks mean left." He was referring to the honking of cars. I didn't quite remember what he said exactly and ended up with both what he said and what my mind made up, which was: *One honk means yes, and two honks mean no.* One day I was in my room. A car drove by the house and honked twice. The sound of honking jumped out at me loud and clear! I immediately thought the car was signaling, "No!" *Is that an objection?* What I was thinking must not have been right. I heard another honk following my reaction. In my head, I reacted to the one honk and understood it be to be, "Yes!" *Whoa, I guess that confirms it.* I didn't look out the window to check who was driving by or what kind of cars they were. I just listened and made sense of the different honking sounds. Honking from that point on became a signal I understood automatically. If a honking lined up with my thoughts, then it provided input.

This felt like a game. I was still working during the day. After work, I was mostly alone. All kinds of sounds started popping up that hadn't before, and I was amazed. Typical background noises became prominent foreground sounds. My brain reacted to these sounds around me instinctively. I was learning a new language that only I knew about. My brain invented with ease and learned fast. I heard sounds that had always been part of my daily life more vividly: honking and car engines, ambulance sirens, pacing and walking upstairs, doors slamming, and helicopters flying. They all had their own special meanings. For example, when I heard a car engine starting, I heard, "Good job!" or "Let's get started." Pacing and running sounds from the ceiling meant, "Keep it up! You are on the right track." An emergency siren meant I needed medical attention or to go to the hospital, or I was doing something crazy or stupid.

One day, Joe was around. I wanted to read a book. I opened the book and heard an ambulance driving by with its siren on. The siren was telling me to stop reading. So I put down the book and pondered what I should do next. I felt a light touch next to my mouth and thought it was Joe telling me to smile. I smiled. I moved closer to the window and looked outside. A helicopter flew by, and I agreed, *Yes, Joe is amazing.* I decided to leave the house for a walk.

In addition to sounds, I also learned special signs from people's gestures, which I had never noticed before. If a person touched her eyebrow, she was telling me, "Open your eyes." If she was touching her nose, it meant: "You are onto something." Touching her ear meant: "Listen." Touching the top of her head meant: "Remember" or "Remember?" Touching her mouth meant: "Smile."

As I walked on the streets in my neighborhood, I noticed the gestures of strangers. Cars passed me by and honked. Another car started its engine right as I walked by. An ambulance drove by with its siren turned on. I tried to walk normally, but all of these sounds came at me one by one, not letting me walk in peace. My brain didn't filter anything out like it should have. It seemed that the outside world was very eager to tell me things or ask me to do things. My brain stayed in this super-alert mode, trying to process what everything meant. Every second held another interruption. Everything I saw was another puzzle to keep track of and figure out. Certain gestures would be stuck in my mind for days or even weeks.

Another person walked by and touched the right side of his mouth. I thought it was a clear message for me: "Smile and don't worry!" I tried to ignore the strangers, their signs, the reactive thoughts in my head and keep walking. I thought to myself, *If you really want to say something to me, say it with your mouth, the normal way!* I didn't participate in the signals or send signals back even though I understood this new language. Before writing all this down, I didn't actually think much about these signals. I'm surprised I wasn't scared to go outside.

After the sounds and signals came, piling on top was the new sensation of being touched. One day as I was walking around in a mall, shopping, I felt a poke on my butt. My brain translated that to, "Hey, look here, talking to you!" I looked around to see if there was anyone looking for me. I thought I might have been touched by a laser pointer. I didn't see any red dot on me. Again, like the voices, I didn't know how this was possible but had no doubt I had just been poked by someone.

A poke was easier to ignore than the warm tingling feelings I started getting from my stomach to my chest. One time I was thinking about Joe while riding the bus to work. I was trying to figure out again why he was around. All of a sudden, a mild tingling pulse went through my upper body. I'd never experienced any such sensation before. I sat there shocked and didn't dare move. Like the voices, I felt that someone was communicating with me. After that, every time I felt embarrassed or very happy, I felt a similar wave.

Somehow I was able to keep my work and personal lives completely separate. At work, voice-free and noise-free, I was able to focus and complete what I needed to do. Outside work, life was abnormal, but it didn't feel that way to me yet. I just kept on going and trying to figure it all out as if there was logic behind everything I was noticing around me at the time.

There was no limit to what I could experience. My brain was the limit.

# 2

# A RUNAWAY MIND

## Summer 2002

### NEW START

The summer before I heard from Joe, I was in a very happy mood. I had just finished a three-week tour in Europe and had a great time. As I stated earlier, I'd been laid off from my first job that year, which gave me a chance to take a longer break from work, and I was alone, without a boyfriend for the first time in nine years. Even though my boyfriend Chris and I had broken up, we were still friends. I had met him in college when we were both in the same master's program, though I was only a senior. After college, I moved to Boston and got a job with the same company as him. We'd lived together for eight years, but he still did not want to get married, which I thought meant he did not love me enough. After we broke up, he continued to keep an eye on me for a while. Our couple-ness lingered. He would call, and we would have dinner together, see movies of his choice, or hang out at the mall. We were mostly comfortable with each other.

Starting my second job, I felt very much recharged. At the new job, I listened to music and unintentionally sang out loud in my cubicle. I chatted with coworkers and laughed so loudly that people down the hall could hear me. That was me without any stress after a six-month break from working. I was able to be myself from the inside out. I felt like a child, completely open-minded and trusting. But even though this was a time when I felt healthy and happy, I also see that perhaps being completely "inside out" made me more vulnerable than I ever was. I was not guarded at all when my mindset started to change quickly after this period, and I started to have such a vivid inner life. I believe that, starting with listening to music, the following seemingly normal and unimpressive events caused and triggered my first voice Joe, which officially made me a schizophrenic. I've gone over this sequence of small and large events many times to understand how they might have altered and stressed my brain in a new way that it had not experienced before.

## MUSIC

A couple of months before I first heard from Joe, I became obsessed with music. A friend told me about Yahoo LAUNCH-cast, which is an online personalized radio. In a couple of hours, I had ranked hundreds of songs. I kept ranking songs, first sitting at my desk, sitting on my bed, and then lying in my bed. I ranked songs until I fell asleep without changing into my pajamas. After a few days of this, the online radio became pretty good at playing songs I liked. I listened to music at work, at home, at the gym, and between work, home, and gym—basically whenever I could.

Then music became slightly more than just music to me.

One day, I was in my room alone as usual. It was in the

middle of winter. I was missing my friends. Not using my computer to listen to the online radio, I turned on the black boombox in my room and I heard a song I really liked. A phrase of the song stood out and echoed in my head. Something about winter. I smiled to myself. I turned to the radio and kneeled down on the floor so I was eye-level with the radio. I'd heard this song so many times before, but this time it felt different. It felt like someone was talking to me through the song, and this person, a man, knew exactly what I was feeling. It was brief, but I felt understood by him. Afterwards, I didn't think more of this sensation and continued with my day.

On a different day, I went to Star Market, a grocery store, to buy chicken breasts for dinner. I was planning to make mushroom chicken soup that night. At the grocery store, there was pop music playing. I walked to the frozen meats aisle, then I went to pay. I did not really acknowledge the music until again, a phrase from a song caught my ears while I was standing in line. Once again, I felt understood. There was that feeling of connection and amazement. I looked around me and noticed that no one was paying any attention to me, and I smiled to myself. It felt like I'd just heard a secret message specifically meant for me. I left the grocery store walking on air.

This continued to happen as I went to different places, from song to song, phrase to phrase. I was amazed each time. It felt magical! I didn't question these feelings. I welcomed them after being surprised by them. The phrases I heard always applied perfectly to me.

One Saturday afternoon, I turned on the radio and a good song was playing. I thought, *Wow. For me? For me! Incredible. That is exactly what I'm feeling. You took the words right out of my mouth. I can't believe this is happening again.* This time I was not only amazed, but I was also curious and thought a step further. I thought, *Who is doing this to me? How do you know what I like? How do you know I am here and am listening right now? How do you surprise me and make me happy again and again?* As I felt a surge of happiness like many times before, my mind was hypersensitive. A wave of sensation was going through my head, and I got the distinctive feeling of someone being out there. I felt special connecting with someone again. It was a very subtle reaction, but this time I automatically jumped to wondering about a person behind the music. I look back to this moment as the first time I had a delusional thought—my mind then became very stuck in this thought pattern and kept repeating itself.

## DAN

Before Joe the voice, there was Dan the coworker at my new job.

In early winter, my company hosted a holiday party in the atrium, a large open space in the middle of our building. As I walked in, I saw a sea of strangers. Holiday music was playing softly in the background. Everyone was dressed festively in gold, red, and black. I stood at the entrance, not sure if I wanted to enter. I panicked slightly. I thought I'd rather hang out with my books. I'd forgotten how to meet new people. I'd been comfortable hanging out with the same friends for six years, with my boyfriend Chris, and at my first job, and now I was okay living my life alone. I was okay starting a new job, meeting new work friends and discussing our software products, but I wasn't sure what to say when people approached me and asked simple questions about my name, where I was from, and what I did for fun. It had been so long since I'd had to make these introductions.

I looked around for the few people I knew at the company. I walked toward a man I knew through the tightly packed sea of people.

"Hi, you made it!" my new coworker said to me.

"Hi," I said. Champagne and hors d'oeuvres were being handed out. I took a glass and ate a quiche. My friend started talking to a friend of his. I stood inside the small circle we made. "Nice party, huh?"

"I'm surprised so many people showed up."

"Yeah, it's not bad. Not bad at all." I didn't say anything. I didn't know how to contribute. I felt so hot and uncomfortable in my red turtleneck sweater. People around me were hitting me with their elbows. I couldn't breathe easily.

"How is the food?" someone said.

"I like that one!" someone else said.

I stood quietly next to my work acquaintances. I tried to keep smiling. Another person joined us. He faced me and introduced himself. "Hi. My name is Steve. What's yours?" It took a few seconds to react. I answered softly, which must have been hard to hear because he asked me again, "What is it?"

I couldn't keep up even with this simple conversation. I couldn't stand how awkward I felt. "I have to go to the bathroom," I said and excused myself and found a quiet spot in the hallway away from the crowd. The fresh air felt so good. I relaxed a bit.

While I was cooling down, I noticed someone walking toward me. I recognized the young man from work. I remembered him from my interview. He'd been standing next to a cubicle when I was leaving the room. He was tall and attractive. He must have noticed that now I was hiding from the party.

Dan stopped in front of me and stood there. He smiled down at me. I looked up at him but stayed quiet. I was not sure what to do. "Did your mother cover you under a blanket when you were a baby?" he said.

*What?* I didn't quite understand what he meant. I felt

embarrassed and awkward again. I wanted to run away. I smiled politely and quickly got up and walked away.

When I got home that night, I became very upset with myself for not responding to Dan. It had all happened so quickly. How could I just stand there and not say anything? Where were my words? What was wrong with me? What was he even saying about me? His casual comment seemed so pointed to me. I cared so much about what he said that I ruminated on it all night. I thought: *He should not have said that to me. We don't even know each other.* In my head, I thought through all the clever responses I could have had.

The next day I went to work with the single thought of correcting Dan. I knew where he sat and went straight there. "Hey," I said.

"Hey," he responded. He didn't look surprised to see me. The two of us stood in the middle of the office. No one else was around. To Dan, who was almost a stranger, I said loudly, almost yelling, "About what you said last night, I don't know what you said about me. You should not say anything about me!"

This time, he was the one who was speechless. I could feel my heart pumping fast. He made me both anxious and excited at the same time. But I didn't say anything else. I left him alone in the room.

Looking back now, I realize I was no longer the healthy and happy version of myself. I had become sensitive and fragile. I had never talked to or yelled at anyone in this way before, especially to a stranger and colleague. But I didn't pick up on my unusual behavior at the time. I just tried to survive it when the awkwardness came.

Like music, Dan became a fixation in my mind. I didn't seek him out, but I felt he kept showing up at the same time and place as me. We worked and worked out at the same small places. We both lived near work and took public transportation. It wasn't difficult to run into him, yet running into him felt surprising and special. It felt intentional, just like the phrases from all those songs. I ran into him almost every day.

I had been keeping to my routine and going to the gym, a small local Cambridge place. My company had a special membership agreement with them. After work, there was usually a rush of people. The first time I tried one of the weight-lifting machines, I couldn't figure out how to adjust the seat. Then I noticed Dan watching. I walked over to him. "Hey! Can you help me? How do I lower the seat?" He came over, showed me how to adjust the seat, and then walked away. He didn't say anything to me. I felt bad that I had bothered him. I wished that we had chatted, that smart words would have flown out of my mouth, that he had wanted to stay longer.

Another night after work, a few of us went to see a friend performing at a nearby bar. I sat alone listening to the music. I was impressed with anyone who could sing and perform. I wanted to show my support. When the performance was done, I went over to my singer-writer friend to say goodbye. Dan was also there. "That was great. Thanks for inviting me! I'm going to go," I said to my friend.

"Why don't you hang around a bit?"

"No. I should really go."

"What do you have to do at home?" Dan jumped in.

I thought, *Ugh. I don't know.* I didn't answer him. I waved goodbye to everyone, turned around, and left the bar. When I had a moment to myself, I wondered why I didn't stay. I knew I liked Dan. On my way home, I kept seeing Dan in my head. A pretty woman was sitting next to him. I told myself, *He definitely has other pretty women as friends.*

Another time, I was invited by my new friends at work to go

to karaoke. On the way there, near Faneuil Hall, Dan showed up. This time when we ran into each other again, it felt like he sought me out. He stood in front of me and asked, "Do you want to come with me to a bar?" I didn't know what to say. I just looked at him. He said, "How about this? We can flip a coin for it. Heads or tails?" He took out a quarter from his pocket and started flipping it.

I quietly said, "I can't," and walked away from him back to my friends. I already had plans. I couldn't ditch my new friends.

Every time I interacted with Dan, I got really anxious. I felt vulnerable and exposed. I noticed his every move, every word. I analyzed them again and again. I drove myself crazy. I had never behaved like this. Later on, I would look back and think, *What would have happened if I had stayed at the bar and hung out with everyone that night? What would have been next if I had said something smart during those chance meet-ups with Dan or gone to a bar with him?* Tension that had nowhere to go was building up inside of me. I took the memories and twisted them in my mind, so I was all knotted up. Before Dan, I was always able to proudly say I had no regrets in life. I was able to move to the United States from Taiwan as a teenager, study and graduate from Cornell, become an independent adult in Boston, and work at challenging companies successfully, but now I couldn't talk to a peer? At the time, I didn't know what to do with my feelings. My behavior was inconsistent and led me to the opposite of what I had wanted to do, which was to get to know Dan better. If I hadn't had a crush on Dan and was not in this frame of mind, my first voice might not have been Joe, a young man just like Dan but imaginary.

# 3

# A BREAKDOWN

Winter 2002

## A NIGHT CRY

After I heard from Joe and learned my new language, on the outside I was doing okay, but deep inside signs of trouble started to show. I was most vulnerable when I tried to fall asleep. First, my conscious mind relaxed and let go. It stopped being in control after holding myself together so tightly during the day, at work, in the evening. My mind started to wander on its own through everything I had experienced. My fear and insecurity surfaced briefly, then I'd fall asleep.

Once I fell asleep, I lost control. I woke up in the middle of the night crying once. As soon as I gained consciousness, I realized there were tears streaming down my face. Confused, I tried not to make any sounds as not to wake anyone else in the house. While my body cried, my mind was a blank. I didn't feel sadness nor was I upset. My body must have been expressing fear buried underneath my toughness without my conscious mind. I wiped my eyes and went back to sleep. I didn't reach out to anyone because I didn't recognize I needed help. I didn't feel badly when I awoke. In my mind, I was still trying to live a productive life and become a stronger person. My stress built up slowly over time through many little events that were almost nothing on their own: the songs, Dan and Joe, the sounds and signals I understood only intuitively. My brain was not doing well at all, but I didn't even remember I had cried in my sleep until many years later.

In 2002, on Halloween day, I walked home from work alone. I went straight to my room on the second floor. All of a sudden, from nowhere, I started crying uncontrollably. I sat in the dark, letting the tears come out. I tried to be very quiet and still, but I must have disturbed my housemate John. He opened my door and kneeled next to me. He put his hand on my arm. Neither of us said anything. I stopped crying. It was nothing. I was fine. Then John left the room, and I went to bed.

Then Christmas came. I was alone in my room again on Christmas Eve. At this point, I was feeling slightly unwell. I was lying in my bed but awake. John came and said, "Come with me." I didn't know where he was taking me, but I followed him. He drove for a while, and we ended up at his family's house in Rockport, Maine. His family welcomed me, and I celebrated Christmas with them without them asking me any questions. They even gave me a gift. John's mother let me stay in their guest room. But I felt uneasy. My mind was anxious. I didn't say a word the whole time other than "Thank you."

## WORK

Work was the last safe space left for my brain. My brain had the chance to reset to normal thoughts and activities during work no matter how crazy or anxious I'd had been the night or weekend before. One day, though, I started to feel all of my coworkers were more energetic. I sent off requests through email. People were more coordinated and efficient than they usually were. It seemed they could read my mind and were responding too quickly, quicker than I expected. I would send an email out and get a response back seconds later. It didn't feel normal. *Is someone able to look at my screen from another computer monitor and read my email? Is that how everyone is so efficient? Is there some sort of training program going on at work? Why did that man walk over, tap dance a bit, and walk away? That seemed weird. Is Joe working with someone at my job now?* A door slammed loudly. I reacted to the sound. *Did I say something wrong?*

There was no normal part of my life now. I felt unusual energy at work, at the gym, and at home. I felt it on the train. Everywhere. After work, I went home. I still was not worried even though I was falling apart quickly. *Calm down*, I told myself.

By now, the man I'd come to call Joe was talking to me every day and every night. Any sound could mean something, could be a sign or a message. It was mentally intense. It was as if I had hundreds of puzzles in my mind, and I was trying to solve them all simultaneously. *What is the message in this movie? Who could possibly be running around town after me? Who is talking to me? Does this person want to hurt me?* My thoughts were happening so fast that my talking felt slow. My brain was so crowded I did not have a second of quietness between thoughts. I could not sleep because of Joe's talking, because of my thoughts.

## ASKING FOR HELP

In January 2003, about two months after I first heard Joe, it was late at night on a Saturday. I was alone again in my house in East Cambridge. I was extremely anxious and could not sleep.

I was pacing in my room. It might have been a couple of days since I'd last fallen asleep. I wasn't worried about not sleeping. I didn't pay any attention to it and didn't keep track of how long it had been. I was focused on listening to Joe talking. I didn't know how long he'd been talking to me. I wanted to ignore him, but I couldn't. Even though I wasn't worried about the insomnia, I recognized I was having a very hard time. I tried to distract myself. I picked up a colored pencil on my desk and started to draw, something that had once calmed me. My right hand shook slightly as I held the colored pencil. I stopped after a few minutes. It was not helping.

Imagine fragmented thoughts and a voice speaking continuously on an infinite loop. Imagine not being able to sleep for days. Imagine not being able to speak because the brain is so overwhelmed with thoughts and the voice that the rest of the body can't function. I couldn't talk at all. I moved slowly. I felt my brain burning and smelling of smoke.

*I really need to get help.* I thought of Chris, my old boyfriend. He'd made me feel safe and comfortable with his mild manner and sound logic. He would know what to do and who to call. Around four o'clock in the morning, I dialed his number, the only phone number I knew by heart besides my own. "I need help. Can you come?" I said. My voice didn't sound like mine. I thought it sounded strange. It didn't take Chris a long time to arrive. Maybe ten minutes. He rang the doorbell, and I met him at the door. It was so good to see him even though I had no idea how I would explain to him what was happening to me.

"Are you okay?" Chris asked calmly while we both stood in the same spot where I'd first heard Joe's voice. The street was dimly lit. My mind heard Chris clearly. However, my body was no longer in my control. I said nothing.

"Are you?" he asked a second time. I just stared at him.

As he helped me into his car, I wanted to ring the doorbell of my next-door neighbor. *Have they been talking to me?* I moved very slowly. Chris didn't look worried, but I found out later he was extremely scared.

I completely relaxed after getting into his car, a familiar thing to do. Joe did not follow me to Chris's apartment. I finally slept. I might have slept for a whole weekend. Then Chris and Jennifer woke me up. "We're going to take you to see a doctor. Come on." My mind was dizzy, blurry, and heavy. The two of them helped me get into the car again. I remember my scarf falling to the ground. Jennifer picked it up and put it back around my neck.

Chris first took me to see his primary care doctor. I hadn't been good about getting annual check-ups and didn't have a doctor of my own. Dr. Stephen was an older man who ran his own private office near Chinatown. He answered the phone himself. He was a family friend of Chris's.

The three of us sat in Dr. Stephen's office. He asked Chris and Jennifer a few questions. I vaguely heard "voices," "can't talk," "she hasn't been like this for very long." Then we drove to a hospital. Dr. Stephen had given us a referral to someone he knew would see me right away.

When I met Dr. Han for the first time, Chris and Jennifer were sitting next to me. Dr. Han was a stereotypical Asian doctor. He didn't offer any polite or friendly greeting. He saw us in his square office at a hospital near Chinatown. His room was filled with piles of paper and binders. He didn't have a receptionist, assistant, or nurse. He started asking questions, speaking with an accent. I heard both Chris and Jennifer tell him I'd been hearing voices. Chris mentioned my mother had schizophrenia. Yes, I had been working before and was normal.

There weren't any windows in that room. Near the ceiling,

there were tiny clicking sounds, kind of like stars blinking. Dr. Han, Chris, and Jennifer talked for a short while, and then the three of us left. Apparently, it was very obvious to the doctor what was happening to me. This was when it was officially decided I was mentally ill and when I was labeled *a schizophrenic* to my close friends, but not to myself yet.

I have no memory of what happened next. I don't remember going back to Chris's home or Chris and Jennifer picking up my prescription on the way back to my old apartment and helping me take it. I know I slept for days. The medication Dr. Han prescribed completely shut me down.

— Part 2 —

# ME

# 4

# MY BEGINNINGS

## 1973 to 2002

### MY PARENTS

My parents married young, in their early twenties. My dad's cousin introduced them to each other. Traditionally, in Taiwan, there is a concept called "matching doors" when two people are considering getting married. My parents' doors were considered well matched, which meant their families had similar social and economic statuses. The marriage was not so much based on love as it was on financial security.

Since the first day they were married, my parents fought frequently, my dad once told me. I was too young to understand their arguments early on, but ever since I could remember my mother was constantly challenging my dad. She was often unhappy and unsatisfied. She told me she'd grown up in a large family with five brothers and two younger sisters, and her father was fairly militant. He often compared his three daughters. He told my mother she was neither pretty nor a good cook, an indirect way of saying she would be useless when she grew up. She channeled all her energy toward her education and her career as a college teacher. She was ambitious and driven despite her father's lack of encouragement or support. In some ways, she was like her father. She had a quick, hot temper and strong personality, which was exactly the opposite of my dad's mild manner. One day at home, I heard loud yelling from my mother. She didn't like something Dad had done. After a series of verbal complaints, out of anger and frustration, Mother flipped the glass tabletop in the living room. The glass was thick and didn't break. Dad cleaned up after her and then walked away, just as I had seen him do many times before.

I was also a person my mother was unhappy with. However, unlike my dad, I was too little to walk away. I don't remember what I did one day. I was about four or five, and my mother was very upset with me and took out an ivy branch and started hitting my small legs with it, which made long and thin red marks. I cried quietly and tried not to make a sound. When I was younger than six, my mother told me to wash the dishes after dinner. I couldn't even reach the sink and had to stand on a little stool. When I first started going to kindergarten, I walked to school by myself in fearful tears. I have very few memories of my mother when I was young, but I remember how she made me feel. I was usually afraid, upset, or crying. Raising a child to be independent is good. However, the way I was taught to be self-reliant was without any warmth.

There was more hidden in my mother's genes. I remember that when I was perhaps five or six, one of my mother's younger brothers didn't have a place to live and came to live with us temporarily. One day, without any warning, he got upset, got hold of a kitchen knife, and cut my mother. I ran out of the house by myself. Later, I learned my uncle had had mental health issues from a young age. I don't know if a doctor ever treated him. I never saw my uncle again. I also learned that one of mothers' aunts killed herself. Another brother of my mother was not well. No one talked openly about these illnesses—I believe this reticence was cultural.

When I was seven years old, my mother left home to study in New York City. She wanted to be a school principal, not just a schoolteacher. Her latest master's degree from the Philippines wasn't enough. She needed a higher degree in order to compete with men. At that time in Taiwan, a married woman with a young child would not normally leave home for her career, but my mother did. I was relieved to be separated from her. She was too dominant and aggressive for me and made constant demands. In addition, the stress and pressure I experienced at a very young age may have affected my brain development. It's hard to judge now.

I have two photographs from my childhood, both from a family trip to the southern part of Taiwan. My parents had taken turns taking pictures with me in a bamboo garden. In one picture, I'm standing in a pink dress with a serious expression next to my tall mother. She's holding one of my hands. I'm not smiling, and neither is she. In the second picture, in the same exact location, my dad is squatting down, holding me in front of him. I have a big grin on my face. I'm cuddling with my father, leaning back into him. He is smiling too.

Starting in second grade, I didn't see or talk to my mother for seven years. She became a stranger in the distance, who sometimes wrote me harsh letters demanding my immediate response or there would be serious punishment whenever she next saw me. I must have benefited from her absence.

## MOVING TO AMERICA

My life changed in a significant way when I was fourteen. A few weeks after the new fall semester started, I sat in my Chinese Literature class with a room of girls my age. In middle school, we all had to cut our hair short—it couldn't be longer than one centimeter below our ears—and we had to wear uniforms. We were separated from the boys, who were on the other side of the building. Uniformity, discipline, and obedience were taught and valued. Out of the blue the teacher called my name, and there was my mother at the front of the room. I hadn't talked to her since she'd left Taipei for America. She looked the same, tall and slender, serious and decided. We didn't talk to or smile at each other, and there was no warm embrace. My classmates looked at me curiously. Some of them knew my mother had been in America, but they knew nothing more than that. I followed her, and we walked out of my middle school in the middle of a Friday. With that, she transferred me out. I didn't get much of a chance to say goodbye to my friends. I didn't even know she was coming that day. We walked home in silence. When we got home, she asked me how my English was, and I said, "I don't know."

Dad had left for America six months earlier. He told me his trip was temporary. He had to help my mother. Then Mother showed up.

The next day I was at the airport with Mother. Everyone, including my grandparents, uncles, aunts, and cousins, was there to send us off to America. No one cried. No one hugged. The Taiwanese culture is not a touchy one. We showed affection by just being there. No one said anything. If someone argued with my mother for taking me away, I was not told. Besides, both my parents were in America now. From the traditional Taiwanese perspective, I belonged with my parents.

I slept through my first ride in a plane. The next thing I remember, I was in a yellow cab in New York City, my first time in a different country. The buildings in New York were so much taller and more impressive. I looked outside the cab and up to see the buildings covering most of the sky. There weren't any motorcycles crowding the streets. There weren't any small street vendors lined up on the sidewalks. Even though I was no longer in an all-Taiwanese city, I was not bothered by this new setting. As a kid, it didn't affect me at all that people looked different from me, and I did not feel like I was in a foreign city or out of place. My mind just digested this new world.

The cab stopped in front of a stone building on West 120th Street. My mother was a full-time student at Columbia University, and my new home was the dorm for graduate students. I followed my mother onto an elevator to the second floor. It was one of the first times I'd ever taken an elevator. I saw my dad. I was happy to see him again. I realized I'd missed him terribly. Dad had gotten a job working as an engineer. It didn't pay well, but it was something. Everything my parents owned was now crammed into a single room. I had my own small room. I hadn't brought much. We had a roommate, a woman from Japan. I'd never lived with a stranger before. I thought the kitchen in the hallway was so tiny. That was the best we could do. Dad kept saying, "Don't worry. This is temporary." My memory of the rest of this day was fuzzy and blurry.

The world I knew had disappeared over one plane flight. I was given a new name my mother said would be easier for everyone here to say and remember. I didn't know any English and didn't know anything about Manhattan or America. But I was here.

On Monday, my mother took me to a middle school near where we lived, Booker T. Washington Junior High School 54. My mother told me, "You should be in a school where no one speaks Chinese. You'll be forced to learn English and learn this new way of living." The new school looked very different from my old school. No one wore uniforms. Girls didn't cut their hair short. Boys and girls were not separated. Instead of wooden tables and chairs, they were metal. Instead of studying all day in the same room, the students had to move to rooms for different subjects and teachers. I felt overwhelmed, but all I could do was keep my eyes open and take everything in. I walked from classroom to classroom, not understanding a word people said. A loud bell sounded around noon, and everyone disappeared. I stood in the middle of the empty hallway alone, and I finally panicked. Tears streamed out of my eyes and down my cheeks. I didn't know where to go. Luckily, a teacher walking by saw me and took me to the school cafeteria.

Other than that one cry, I never felt fear as a kid. As a teenager, I tried to fit in and adapt. I just let go of my experience in Taiwan and started a new life in America. I was naturally positive and forward-looking. The first few years I lived in New York City, I wrote letters to my family and friends back in Taiwan, but slowly the number of letters decreased and then stopped. My English became better. After being mute for a month or so, I started speaking English. I was lucky to meet some great teachers and kids. I was the first Asian student they'd ever had at the school, and they welcomed me with open arms. I made new friends and started to enjoy life in the Big Apple. I learned to lean on teachers and friends, my new village, while my parents worked and studied.

When I was older, I found out the reason for our move to America. My mother had triggered her schizophrenia while studying alone in New York City. She was having a hard time with professors. She thought someone was tapping her conversations. She heard voices when she was alone. She realized it was abnormal, so she checked herself into a nearby hospital. Even though she could walk to the nearby hospital emergency room on her own, she was not at peace with her condition. This began a long struggle of her being on and off medications and going in and out of her doctorate program. Schizophrenia was the reason I had come to America.

In New York, my mother, my father, and I lived fairly independent lives from one another. Mrs. Capaldi, a librarian at the school, became my mother figure. She took a special interest in me and pointed out to other teachers that it did not make sense for me to take on a foreign language since I needed to learn English. While other students were studying French or Spanish, she let me hang out in the library. She suggested easier books for me to read. She let me organize the books. She often took time to chat with me. Because education was always important to my mother, when I took a statewide exam and didn't get into one of the top three high schools in New York, she found a prestigious public high school in New Jersey, where she wanted me to move right away. Mrs. Capaldi contacted my mother and expressed her concern. She wanted me to finish the last year of middle school with my friends. I started living with Mrs. Capaldi during the weekdays while I finished middle school with my friends. We had dinners together. After dinner, Mrs. Capaldi always asked me how my day was at school. During weekends, she took me to museums, parks, and shops in New York City. She told me once that if I were to become an American, I needed to know what other people were talking about. During this time, I was mostly shielded from my mother and her struggle with schizophrenia.

Once I started going to high school in New Jersey, I lived in a house with my parents and could see how my mother was living. She often paced back and forth in her tiny study in the back of the house. The study was filled with books and papers. If she was not in her study, she was in her bedroom napping.

We hardly ever spoke to each other. I spent my time with books and new friends from school. I made spending money by babysitting and tutoring kids in the neighborhood. During weekends, I went out with friends. I was still pretty separated from my mother's journey. She kept to her study and bedroom while I kept to my room.

The rock in my life was my dad. Dad was tall, thin, and fairly handsome. Our ancestry might have involved interracial marriages with Western immigrants to Taiwan because my father had a nose that was considered Western. I wished I'd gotten his nose. Even though Dad and I did not spend much time together, I saw how he lived. When I was alone, I often thought of him. I noticed how hard he worked. He spent only eight hundred dollars for his first car in New York City and drove that car for as long as he could, for more than ten years. I learned to keep quiet and work hard too. "We should be thankful that I have a job to support us," he said to me once. Unlike Mother, who was always trying to change me every time we interacted, my dad accepted me unconditionally.

## OLIVER AND MOTHER

My senior year in high school I applied to Cornell because of its size, its women's fencing team, its beautiful campus, and its excellent engineering program. I didn't want to run out of people to meet, and Cornell seemed like a great college with a large student body. I wanted to keep fencing after high school. I was accepted to Cornell and spent the next four and half years in Ithaca studying electrical engineering and engineering management.

My college boyfriend Oliver and I knew each other through the Taiwanese club though he was two years ahead of me, and we didn't have any classes together. Always upbeat, Oliver often said hello with a big smile. He was tall for a Taiwanese American. He was intelligent and organized and never had any trouble with his classes. In high school, he already knew what he wanted to be when he grew up, a doctor. Oliver planned to marry a nice girl and raise happy kids. He won me over by showing me how much he loved spending time with me. Under a waterfall, we had our first kiss. I was often surprised by flowers from him. We sang karaoke together. We understood how exciting bubble teas were. He kept an eye on my classes as well. A bit nerdy, he wanted to take care of me whenever and however he could. He talked about our future often. We were each other's many firsts.

While I was in Ithaca and a sophomore, I got an unexpected call from one of Mother's friends in Millburn. "You have to come and get your mother out of my house! Hurry! Someone has to deal with this situation." She didn't say anything more. I didn't know what was going on. If this woman hadn't called, I probably wouldn't have ever known something was wrong because my parents never called me. That was how the three of us—Dad, Mother, and me—had always lived, independently and separately. I told Oliver about the call, and he decided to drive us to New Jersey right away.

When we arrived, I found out my mother was no longer living with my dad. She had moved out and was crashing at different places. At this time, she was living in the basement of a friend's. She didn't speak much to anyone anymore and was always deep in her own thoughts. She hid in the basement most of the time. When Oliver and I arrived, my mother was packed up and ready to leave. She was quiet and serious. She might have been thinking hard about something. She wasn't surprised to see me. The first thing she said was that she wanted a ride to the airport, so she could fly back to Taiwan. It was clear she wanted help leaving. I had no idea if she had purchased plane tickets. Her friend told me Mother was carrying a knife in her bag. I thought she carried it to protect herself and was not afraid of her. My dad was with me, but he was hiding out in the car. I got the impression from him that she really wouldn't want to see him. Dad's suggestion was that we drive my mother to a hospital in Manhattan, where she had once gone for appointments.

Oliver loaded my mother's suitcases into his sedan. Every available space in the car was occupied—that was how much stuff she had with her. The three of us, including my mother, got into Oliver's car and left her friend's. Her friend looked relieved. She definitely wanted Mother to be out of her house. My dad followed from a distance as Oliver drove, leading us all to Manhattan. I'd never gone to this hospital with my mother, but I knew where it was. We stopped the car on the Upper West Side. Of course, my mother wasn't aware of our plan.

"Okay, I think we're here," I said to Oliver. We looked at each other and got out of the car. My mother looked preoccupied as she followed us.

There was a man walking by. Oliver walked over to him. I could hear his hushed voice. "Hey, man. Can you help me take this woman into the ER?" Oliver asked. The stranger agreed, and Oliver shook hands with the man and gave him ten dollars. The two of them walked over to my mother. Each grabbed one of her arms and started guiding her toward the emergency room.

"Aaaahhh! No! Aaaaah! Nooooo!" My mother finally caught on and started screaming at the top of her lungs. Quickly, Oliver and the stranger reacted and picked up my mother and carried her into the ER. I followed them. When my mother was inside, my dad walked toward us from his parked car on the other side of the street.

The hospital staff took her in. My dad hovered at the entrance. The nurse found my mother's record and admitted her. We didn't have to do any paperwork because they had her information. Then Dad, Oliver, and I left the hospital. Oliver and I went back to Ithaca. Dad went back to New Jersey. I didn't talk to or see Mother again until my graduation from Cornell. I didn't think about finding out what happened to her after we sent her into the ER, how long she had stayed in the hospital, or how she got out. No one ever talked about these things. The hospital incident was just Mother being Mother, and it felt like my mother's life was none of my business. I'd learned as a young child my mother was often angry, and so, as a young adult, I knew again to stay out of her sight.

When we got back to school, Oliver talked to me about my risk of triggering schizophrenia. He'd done some research and told me schizophrenia could be caused by both genetics and environmental factors, such as stress. Since I had a parent with schizophrenia, the probability of my triggering the same illness was significantly higher. Oliver didn't change his mind about going out with me after learning of my mother's illness. Quite the opposite, he said he was prepared to help me manage this new risk. We only talked about it once. I didn't think about it beyond our conversation. I didn't think about it as seriously as Oliver did. I actually didn't think about it at all. I didn't even know what schizophrenia was. This was not at all an important, tangible risk to me. I forgot about it just like I had forgotten my mother was ever in the hospital.

Oliver graduated from college at the end of my sophomore year and went on to medical school in the Midwest. We continued to date long distance. He spoke of marriage often. I felt pressured. I hadn't even graduated from college yet. I ended up breaking it off with him a year later.

## CHRIS

As a senior in college, I met Chris. He was born in Hong Kong, but grew up in a boarding school in Scotland. We both came from families that raised ultra-independent kids. He came to Ithaca alone for college after Scotland. My first impression of him was he was funny, good looking, clean cut, and well groomed. He did not speak with a Scottish accent. I preferred a bookish guy rather than a frat boy. After I got to know him, I found out he was a bit of a nerd and goofy at heart. He was gentle, confident, and smart. We hit it off after he chased me a bit around campus. We started doing homework together for our master's program. We often had healthy debates challenging each other's views. We held our different positions. We often asked each other to explain our ideas.

One day while I was working in the computer lab, Chris talked to me excitedly: "I'm going to play golf. Do you want to come?" I thought he'd asked me a very strange question. I'd never played golf before. Besides, I was working. Seeing my reaction, he quickly changed his question and asked me out to dinner. He took me out in his sports car, which became a routine. On a snowy night, he pulled his handbrake to show me how he could spin his car on the ice. I was happy to see more of him. Pretty soon, we were always together.

During college, Chris adopted a tuxedo kitten whom he named Lupus, which meant *wolf* in Latin. Chris and Lupus were so alike. The only pets I had growing up were palm-sized turtles and fishes in a tank. Chris was happy to introduce me to Lupus, who was a very gentle kitten. I adored the kitten immediately.

Chris taught him to play catch using a foil ball. Lupus also liked to cuddle. We thought Lupus might think he was a dog.

At the end of my senior year, Chris graduated. We left things open and didn't have any discussion about our relationship. He got a pretty good job at a small, fast-growing software consulting company in Boston called Sapient. That summer he picked me up in Ithaca, so I could hang out with him in Boston. Then it was my turn to find a city where I could start my new life. Because of Chris, when I graduated, I ended up moving to Boston and working for the same company as he did. In the next five years, Chris and I spent all of our waking moments together. He often decided on where we would eat and interesting places to visit. He suggested movies and computer games for us. Chris opened my eyes to the world and introduced me to traveling and vacations. He took me on my first cruise to the Cayman Islands and my first trip to Europe. He planned everything for us. Together we attended many weddings. We were surrounded by our couple friends. Sometimes he even helped me with work. We had the same job, understood each other, and were both committed to our work. I felt happy, safe, and comfortable with Chris and finally moved in with him. Our lives were inseparable.

In our early twenties, Chris was more adventurous than me. He liked to explore. He wanted and helped me to do the same. I remember when we were on the cruise to the Caribbean, I saw the spa on the ship. "There's a spa!" I whispered. "I've never had a massage before. Should I try it?"

"Yep. Try it if you want. You make enough. You can afford it!"

"Yeah! Why not?" I said excitedly.

"I'll just wait for you at the library." He flashed me his cutest smile.

I was young and still learning about how to live life. Chris shared with me everything he loved in his life: Lupus, video games, food, movies, travel, and investing. In return, I took charge of our social calendar with friends. We became good friends with Jennifer, Samantha, Paige, Zoe, John, and Ahmed from Sapient. Friendly Jennifer had a full head of brown, curly hair and loved sci-fi movies. Confident Samantha was from Boston and knew the best restaurants. Kind Paige was a vegetarian and was as easygoing as me when it came to hanging out. Unlike everyone else who worked directly with me, passionate Zoe worked on the same project as Chris and often told me about Chris's mischief during the day. Intelligent John was also local, went to school at MIT, and was extremely good at coding. Coolheaded Ahmed was into movies, zoos, and cars. We had a very diverse group of friends from different parts of the world in addition to the States. We were all single and in our early twenties. We worked together, ate dinners together, and spent weekends watching movies and hanging out.

Unlike Oliver who wanted to talk about everything in our relationship, Chris and I, behaving similarly, did not talk about anything related to our bond. With Dad and Mother, I learned to take care of myself and was not in the habit of being communicative about my thoughts and feelings. I also grew up not asking anyone for anything. Marriage, family, kids were not at all on my mind. I think they were not on Chris's mind either for whatever his reasons were. For a long while, we were happy with just being with and having each other.

One thing was clear. We had completely opposite views on medicine and doctors. I'd always been healthy and didn't grow up going to the pediatrician. However, one night, as I was getting ready for bed, my arm brushed against my left breast, and I felt something hard inside. I immediately panicked. I told

Chris, and he called a nurse hotline. The next day Chris took me to see a doctor and later to get a biopsy and later again for a day surgery to remove a cyst from my breast. Luckily, it was a benign cyst. Chris took care of both of our health issues. For eight years, I always had Chris.

One day Chris and I were at home. He was sitting at the dining table while I was sitting on the sofa. A sense of loneliness came up inside for a short second out of nowhere. *Can I be lonely while going out with someone? Is that possible?* "How do you think we're doing?" I asked him.

"What do you mean?" he said.

"We've been going out for a while."

"If you're thinking about marriage, I don't want to get married right now." Silence filled the air between us.

"I think I should move out," I reacted.

"Are you sure?"

"Yes, I think I should move out." Immediately, I felt there was no future for us. My brain reacted logically to protect myself, and I put my emotions aside.

"Okay," he said, not disagreeing or trying to persuade me not to leave.

A few weeks later Chris helped me move out. I started to disconnect my life from his and his from mine, but we still saw each other on and off. My friend Jennifer and her boyfriend had lived downstairs from Chris and me. Jennifer was shocked. She said she and her boyfriend had modeled their relationship stages after us. There was no question Chris and I would be together forever.

I was twenty-eight. I was single for the first time in eight years and not tied to a job, and I felt liberated. My optimistic nature was at work!

## FRESH START

Immediately, I started trying new things. I started running for the first time since elementary school. I started with a few minutes, and then went up to an hour. I was getting better every night. I felt healthy. I started writing for fun every night after running. One thousand words was my daily goal. They were short posts about my life, how I felt about Chris, work, and made-up stories based on what I experienced in the past. I didn't hold back and poured my heart out. I even created a website to share my writing, not really worrying about who was going to read it. I also started reading again because I hadn't read for pleasure since college. I got really interested in how people lived their lives and read many biographies and memoirs. All these new activities filled out my days. I felt focused and energetic. Life was amazing!

# 5

# STEPS FORWARD, STEPS BACK

## 2003 to 2010

## WOKE UP AT CHRIS'S

After taking the medication for the first time, I slowly became conscious. My mind was blank and quiet. No thoughts were running through my head. It felt so good. I was at Chris's home, and both Chris and Jennifer were there. I smiled at my friends, but I didn't say anything. I felt like I'd woken up from a really good night of sleep, but it'd been an entire day.

Jennifer handed me the phone and told me to call my mother. I listened and dialed the number of her apartment. I didn't know the last time I had talked to Mother.

"Hello?"

"Hi, Mother," I said.

"Hi, Mindy."

"I'm hearing voices." This was all I thought to say to her. I started crying.

"Oh, it's okay. It's okay."

Silence. We didn't know how to have a conversation. "Okay.

Bye," I said. I swallowed my emotions and calmed down. I was fine.

"Okay. Take care. Bye."

A few years later, Jennifer told me she wished my mother could have talked to me about what was happening. Jennifer didn't feel like she knew how to help. She thought perhaps Mother could tell me what to do, share her experience, support me. But I was never helped by her. I just blindly made the call and didn't realize at the time I needed to take charge of my own life.

"You must be hungry. Let's get some food in you!" Jennifer then said. She and Chris took me across the street to the Copley Mall. I ordered a burger and some fries at a restaurant called Marche. I hadn't eaten in a couple of days. It might have been longer. I might have forgotten to eat for a day or two when I'd been on my own. My hands were shaking slightly while holding the fries. I opened my mouth to speak, but no words came out. I was used to "talking" without moving my mouth. Fortunately, after a few minutes, my body started working again.

After getting food, we went back to Chris's. Jennifer handed me an envelope. I looked at her, wondering what it was. "It's short-term disability," she said. She'd talked to my manager. She thought I could take some time off to rest. I took the envelope but didn't look at it. I didn't understand why I needed disability. I wanted to go back to work right away. I felt fine. Besides, how could I not work?

I went back to work the next day. I didn't talk to Chris or Jennifer about what had happened. I didn't talk to my mother about the voices again. I didn't tell my dad. I didn't talk to anyone. No one came to talk to me either even though Chris had told our close friends while Jennifer took care of people at work, explaining my brief absence. Some of my friends told me later they were waiting for me to bring up the subject in order to be respectful of my privacy. I didn't know who knew and who didn't. I wasn't intentionally being private. At the moment I just didn't remember any details of my breakdown. I went back to life as if nothing happened.

From this point on, I lived in two separate worlds: the normal world and Joe's world. I was in one or another—they were never mixed together. As if the light was on in a room, when I was with friends and at work, I was able to live my life completely forgetting about Joe's voice, sounds, and signals. I enjoyed being out with friends, making occasional doctor's visits, and working hard, the normal day-to-day stuff. However, when I was alone, it was as if the light had been switched off, and the darkness was "on" in that same room, and the world of Joe's voice and my memories of it, though unspoken, over-powered everything else. When Joe's world was switched on, often late at night, normal thoughts disappeared completely. I became enveloped by the past, feeling stuck with many questions without any answers until I gave up trying to make sense of things and went to sleep.

## DR. HAN

When I had my first follow-up visit with Dr. Han, Chris and Jennifer came with me. I was thankful they did because I had no idea what to say. I didn't grow up with doctors. Even when I was terribly sick as a child and young adult, I would just drink hot water—that was my dad's advice. Even with my lack of experience, I did respect doctors based on my upbringing. When I was in Taiwan, whenever someone was seriously sick, Grandfather or Dad would take that person to see our local doctor. It was always a man. I remember tagging along. It was always the doctor talking. My family just listened and nodded. We would take whatever was prescribed religiously.

I was an awkward patient. Dr. Han started the appointments by asking me how Mother was. I could only answer him, "Fine." I had nothing more to say.

He would then follow up with, "How are you?" I would reply with the same one-word answer. Then he scribbled on a small, square, white piece of paper and handed that to me. "Okay. Here is your prescription." The first time I got a slip I wasn't sure what to do with it. I took it and put it in my bag. I thought to ask Chris and Jennifer about it later.

"Thank you," I smiled politely.

"Anything else?" Dr. Han looked at me and wrote something in his notebook. The appointment was usually finished in less than five minutes. Dr. Han would say he'd see me next time and tell me when to see him next. I was never proactive. However, I never missed my appointments. I kept to them just like I locked my front door at home. Life was good as far as I was concerned. There was nothing to discuss with the doctor. He never changed what he asked me when we met. I treated these visits like I was going to see the doctor for an annual check-up and not like my symptoms were related to any serious mental condition. I don't remember the frequency I saw him at the beginning, probably every few months just so he could refill my prescription. Luckily, I realized years later, a small dosage of Zyprexa was having a great effect on me. Not everyone with schizophrenia was this fortunate. Immediately, the medicine had been able to block out Joe's voice. After a few years, Dr. Han made me see him once a year, which made it pretty easy to forget that schizophrenia was really a part of my life.

Sometimes I think I might have benefited from Dr. Han's hands-off treatment style. I was Dr. Han's patient for eight years, and during those years when I saw him occasionally, I was able to work, hang out with friends, and travel without the worry of having a mental illness. On the surface, I was doing great. On the other hand, no one was helping me to understand what I had gone through and what my future could hold. From my behavior changes and meeting Joe to having my first breakdown, the whole experience remained a mystery.

The only change I made in my life was to take a small, white pill every night before I went to bed. It was the only evidence and reminder that something kind of crazy had ever happened to me.

## BLANK PAGES

I feel extremely lucky I experienced my first psychosis at the age of thirty. My personality was already developed. I'd lived thirty years of stable life. I already had developed professional skills and could support myself financially. I was capable of having relationships with friends, family, and boyfriends. Life would have been perfect, except that certain triggers kept leading me back to an imaginary place.

Even though I was on medication, I didn't understand I had a brain disease. Old memories mixed with new hallucinatory experiences created more disconnected events that, though I could quickly dismiss and forget them, puzzled me more when Joe's world was "on."

After my breakdown, I made new friends at work and was no longer alone most nights. There were six to ten of us who hung out regularly on Thursday, Friday, Saturday, and Sunday nights. At ProfitLogic, I became close friends with Maggie, Nina, Wendy, Andy, and Lani. Agreeable Maggie loved Tom Brady and had a beagle called Brady. Warm Nina was a project manager but had great tastes in fashion and interior design. Foodie Wendy loved running and skiing. Friendly Andy liked to hang out, watch sports, and have a good time. So did sophisticated Lani, who had great dance moves. We'd go to live karaoke nights in Faneuil Hall, trivia nights in the North End, clubs in Back Bay, and bars downtown. I continued to work diligently during the day. My crush Dan had left the company. My short-term awkwardness with people had diminished.

However, sometimes when I was alone at night at home I became vulnerable. One such evening, sitting in front of my desk, I remembered the life I'd lived right before my breakdown. I remembered it as being perfect—I was exercising, reading, and writing. I even had my own blog site that included my made-up stories. Ideas and thoughts came easily to me. I wanted that more creative life back, but I'd locked up my diary. I wanted to go back and read what I wrote. I wanted to know what had happened, but I didn't remember my password. I felt I had overreacted when I'd deleted my blog. I wondered: *Why did I freak out that much?* I couldn't remember exactly what the reasons were.

I wanted to write again. I opened a new document on my laptop. I looked at the blank page. One minute passed. Two minutes passed. Five minutes. My mind was completely blank. Nothing came to me. Feeling frustrated, I closed the blank document on my laptop and gave up. I just felt nothing sitting there. I asked myself, *What happened?* But I had no answer.

The next night I was alone again at home, and I tried again to write. I still could think of nothing even though I placed my fingers on the keyboard, wanting to type. I used to write about what happened during my day, how I felt when I was running on the treadmill, what the people along Charles River looked like on a sunny summer Sunday, what I wished I could learn from my manager at work, plus fiction. Now I didn't have any inspiration at all.

Mixed into my seemingly normal and functional life were visits to Joe's world. I could never move past Joe's world once I was in my alone place. I wanted to make sense of that part of my life. Unfortunately, I had an imperfect memory. I tried to dig deeper each time I remembered Joe's world, but I couldn't write about Joe's world because, at this time, it was completely blank to me. My brain was in a way protecting me from myself. I remembered the first time the voice talked to me, and that was it. There was nothing there in my memory to write about. And now, I had this pill bottle. Why was I taking this pill every night? I thought the pill acted like a switch. When I took the pill, the voices were switched off from some sort of speaker system, and I could not hear Joe. Joe was told to be quiet. Chris and Jennifer knew about the pill, and I trusted my friends. They wouldn't hurt or lie to me. But they must not have known everything I knew, or they would have helped me more. One night I looked at the little, white, round pill and cried. *How did I end up with this?*

Taking medication was useful for blocking out talking voices in my brain. The pill blocked brain receptors that dopamine works on, and schizophrenia is associated with an overactivity of dopamine, which can contribute to hallucinations, such as hearing voices or sounds that are not really there. But, for me, the medicine only affected hearing voices. My memory was not changed nor was my sense of logic. I felt stronger and stronger about being responsible for the thousands of seemingly independent decisions I'd made leading up to my breakdown. If I hadn't freaked out, starting with my experience with Dan, maybe I wouldn't have had a breakdown. If I hadn't had a breakdown, I wouldn't need to take pills. Every time I was alone long enough, I would come to the same conclusion: *I am responsible for what has happened.*

## LIVING ALONE

I wanted to move out of the house in East Cambridge. Whenever a car honked or a siren sounded, I jumped a little. The surrounding noises sounded too familiar, and I didn't like them. I didn't want to keep renting. I'd moved twice already in one year. I was so sick of packing and moving. I decided to buy a place. I wanted to go back to Back Bay, the Boston side of the river. It was easier for someone like me who didn't own a car.

I knew I wanted lots of natural light from big windows. I wanted a fireplace. I wanted brick interior walls. During the first weekend when I started looking, I ran into an open house on Massachusetts Avenue, a small one-bedroom I could call home. It had big windows and lots of sunlight throughout the whole apartment. No fireplace, but it had floor-to-ceiling built-in bookshelves down the long hallway. The apartment was in good condition. I liked the wall colors. I wouldn't need to change anything before I moved in, and it was in my price range. I was excited. *This could work. I could live here.* I'd started reaching out to friends again and told Chris about the apartment.

"You want to buy a place? I don't know what's scaring you or what you're running from, but that's great," he said.

"Would you come and take a look?" I asked him.

"Sure. I'll take a look."

I made an appointment with the selling agent to see the apartment in private. I rented a Zipcar and picked up Chris, Jennifer, and another friend John. We all went to see the place. In 2004, I officially became a homeowner and moved into my own apartment—a big check mark for living my life and achieving an important personal milestone.

I called Dad and told him about the largest purchase I'd made in my life. He was happy for me. A few days later, I received a handwritten letter from him. Since I moved to the US, I hadn't gotten any letters from him. I opened it and unfolded a sheet of white paper. "Congratulations. I'll bring my toolbox to visit you. Love, Dad." I still have this letter with me.

At some point, I heard voices again when I was alone in my new Back Bay apartment. The voices were of the same guy and a new girl. They were talking between themselves. They didn't really bother me. Perhaps my medication was not strong enough, but I didn't know to talk to my doctor or anyone else about it. One day I was reading on my sofa in my living room, and they were chatting, barely audible, above me, near the ceiling. I couldn't make out what they were saying, quite different from Joe. I didn't interact with them. They didn't stay around often or for very long. I didn't think hearing them was strange. They blended into the background, just like all the other noises, the radiators, birds, cars, around the apartment.

There were days when I was more curious and adventurous. One day I heard walking upstairs from above my ceiling. This time I went upstairs to try to find out who was making the sound. I said to myself that maybe this was a good time to visit my neighbor. I was just going to say hi. I wouldn't do or say anything foolish. I knocked on the door upstairs. No one answered. I knocked some more. There was no response. I waited for about ten minutes, then I gave up and came back home.

Later, I mentioned this to Chris. By this time, he had the habit of just dropping by to say hello. He talked to me while he looked around every room in my apartment. I could tell he still cared very much for me, but at the same time he was getting frustrated with how I was not taking care of myself.

"I went upstairs," I told him.

"Why?" he said, as he opened the refrigerator. "Are you eating out a lot or cooking?" I knew he was asking because we used to eat out together for every meal, but now he was trying to cook.

"It sounded like someone walking upstairs. I wanted to find out who was making the noise from the ceiling. I have not started cooking here. I eat out."

Chris looked alarmed. "Don't go upstairs! What's wrong with walking? Are you taking your pills?"

I stood in front of him silently. *Okay.* I could not talk to him about it. *Forget it,* I thought. I felt I couldn't have any proper conversation with him or anyone else about what I really thought and definitely not about the language I'd made up in my mind with signs and sounds. I didn't know how I would even start the conversation.

"Why don't you read about schizophrenia?" It felt like Chris was yelling at me. "I searched online and read about it as much as I could. Your mother has it. Why don't you read about it? Why are you going upstairs? I really don't understand you."

I didn't understand why he was talking about schizophrenia when I was talking about people walking upstairs. I just wanted to see who it was.

"Why? Huh?" He questioned me again.

"I don't know," I said slowly. I didn't say I wanted to find out who was making the noise that drove me crazy, or that, again, I was trying to sort out all the questions in my mind. I was trying to make myself feel better. I was trying to stop the confusion. I didn't know how to tell him why I wanted to go upstairs and talk to the person walking, how I wanted to see if there was a real person there, how someone could talk to me without me seeing that person, how I had so many questions in my mind and was finally looking into trying to explain things logically to myself.

Now Chris was shouting at me. "My sister has MS, and my family is searching so hard for anything that can help her. There's no medication for MS. She can't even take anything if she wanted to. There is no help. Why don't you take your pill? You are lucky!"

I didn't say anything. I was still taking the pill. I didn't correct him. The pill was not a magic silver bullet for everything in my life.

"How is Lupus?" I asked, changing the subject.

"He's good."

"Can I have him?"

"No. He's mine! Okay. I've got to go. Don't go upstairs!" he said as he walked out of my apartment.

I walked him to my door and watched him leave. I felt that he often just stormed in and stormed out for no reason.

I didn't realize it at the time, but I'd made a little progress that day with my trigger. Instead of getting a message from the pacing sound from the ceiling, I wanted to see who was walking around upstairs. My thinking was more clear, and my reaction more reasonable. Perhaps it was the thirty good years I had that were giving me the strength.

## BLACK OUT

My struggle at this stage came in small ways. I would take a few steps toward normality, and then my past would pull me a few steps backwards. For the most part, I didn't tell anyone what was happening to me.

Dr. Han prescribed a sleeping pill, Abilify, in addition to my first regular medication, Zyprexa. For a short period of time, responding to my complaints about weight gain, he also let me try Risperidone for a couple of months. I didn't feel the difference, so he switched me back to Zyprexa. I wouldn't try the sleeping pill for a while. One day I was frustrated with waking up in the dark and being confused by old memories. Without turning on the light, I took a pill from one of the pill bottles. I had three different ones: my previous medication for schizophrenia, my current medication, and the sleeping pill. I was sure I remembered which one was the sleeping pill bottle. A few minutes after I took the pill in the dark, as I was walking around my bed, I must have blacked out and fallen to the floor.

Later, it was bright out. I heard someone knocking on the door as I woke up on the floor at the end of my bed. At first, I didn't understand what had happened. I got up, still feeling a bit dizzy, and opened the door. It was Chris. "Hi. How are you? Is everything okay?"

"I'm fine."

"Okay. I'm going out of town for a few days. I have to catch a plane actually. I'm on my way to the airport." His timing was amazing. *Does he know what just happened?*

"Have a good trip," I said.

Chris went to my kitchen, opened the fridge, closed it, and took a quick walk through my living room while I followed and looked at him curiously. *What's he doing? It's a bit weird.* "You haven't done anything new at your place?"

"No. I have not."

Looking at his watch, he said again he had to go. "Take care of yourself." And he rushed out.

I watched him close the door. I went back to my bedroom and sat at the end of my bed. I was lucky I hadn't hit anything when falling onto the floor. I didn't have any way of finding out if I'd taken the wrong pill but couldn't think of any other reason why I'd blacked out like that—it had never happened before. I was scared. I told myself never to take a pill in the dark again. Since then, I've been keeping old and new medications in separate places to avoid mistakenly taking the wrong pill.

At this point on my schizophrenic journey, Chris was the only person who came and knocked on my door to check on me directly and repeatedly. He might not have known what was best for me, but he came. Because of our past, he didn't have to worry about being intrusive. What I didn't know was that he was also in contact with my friends. He was the second person who talked to me about schizophrenia, after Oliver. But again, I didn't really hear what he was saying. He tried to be helpful, but he was not helping.

## FENWAY

One morning when I woke up, Joe's world was on. Even though it was a work day, I decided to skip work impulsively, find him, and figure everything out. *This is important to me! I am going to do this today.* I left my place and walked under the sun. I was remembering how on other occasions his voice had talked to me so clearly. "I'm going to call you *Joe!*" I said in my head. It was the first name that popped into my mind as I walked south of Massachusetts Avenue toward Newbury Street. I didn't want to call this young man by anyone else's name, and I'd never known a Joe. I liked the name immediately. I looked for signs from Joe. I went to my favorite bookstore cafe. *What does Joe want me to do?* I bought a magnet that said: "Peace starts with a smile." Then I went to a flower shop and bought my favorite flowers, tulips. *Joe would want me to be happy!* When I went home with my magnet and flowers, I realized again that Joe was not going to show up. Disappointed, I sat on my sofa and spaced out. Even though I was taking Zyprexa and was voice-free on this day, I was not willing to let him go in my mind. No medication could make me. Deep down, I still wanted Joe to show himself. Even though I was not hearing from him anymore, I remembered him and felt he was there with me.

One night I sat on my sofa in the living room, listening to my radio. It was playing "I Hope You Dance." I started to get emotional. The radio played "The Middle" next. I listened to the lyrics carefully, as if I was listening to someone talking to me. It said, "Just be yourself. Everything will be alright." I totally agreed. For the next four or five songs, as soon as I heard a line in the music that meant something to me, it brought me back to the middle of my other world.

"Can we meet?" I said to Joe silently in my head. He didn't respond.

I ignored the silence and smiled. I made up my mind. We were going to meet. Today was the day. I so wanted to meet him. I put on my jacket. I rushed out of my apartment. It was around midnight and pitch-dark outside. The next day was a normal workday.

I walked quickly. I didn't know where I was headed, but I knew I could figure it out as I went. I kept on walking in the dark. Another car honked once again. *Left again? Okay. Let's see where I should make a left.* After a few seconds of silence, I knew where I was going. *Fenway Park! What a perfect place to meet,* I thought. I felt a little poke on my back as a sign of agreement.

I stood outside of gate E at Fenway Park and waited. There was no one around. The emotional rush from the music was pretty much gone. A car drove by. The car made a U-turn at the corner outside of gate E and disappeared. I waited and just hoped. I didn't know how long I waited under the stars. After I felt I had waited long enough, I walked home.

On the way home, I heard a voice that said, "Go home."

*I agree*, I thought. *Today is not the day. No big deal.* I went home, turned off the radio, took a shower, and went to bed. And just like that, I left my other world.

Another weekend I was getting frustrated with how I couldn't get anywhere with Joe. I decided to go for a run along the Charles River. I wanted to let out my frustration. It started to rain and then pour. I thought the sky was crying for me even though I couldn't cry. I ran and ran in the rain. I couldn't explain my feelings that night to anyone.


## GIRLFRIENDS

While I was not in Joe's world, which was a good amount of the time, I got in touch with some old friends. Paige emailed me one day. "Do you want to meet up for lunch?" We worked very close to each other.

"That would be great. I'd love to meet up!" I responded with happiness. During lunch, we took turns talking about our lives, work, and home. After that, Paige and I met regularly. I invited more women to join us, Vara and Zoe, both friends from the Sapient days. Instead of lunches, we met after work for dinners or Saturday brunches, as often as their busy schedules allowed.

Most of our conversations focused on taking care of children and husbands. They were also about how we could become better people. One day at brunch, we started discussing swimming. Coincidentally, none of us could swim. Being parents, Zoe and Paige worried about their boys playing in the water. "How do I help them if they get into trouble at the pool?" We decided to tackle swimming and take classes together.

The four of us bought six swimming classes, then six more, and then six more. I had taken swimming lessons when I was little. I could swim, but I didn't know how to play in the water. I was not comfortable in the water. These classes with my girlfriends gave me a bit more confidence each week. We helped each other. After swimming, we had brunch together.

While we were eating once, Zoe said, "Mindy, look at you. So good in the water. Not like us!"

I responded, "I still don't know how to float in the ocean. So I don't consider myself as really knowing how to swim. I'm not relaxed in the water."

Paige smiled. "At least you are swimming!"

Vara agreed, "Yes, at least you're floating in the pool." Vara was so skinny she had a hard time floating.

We continued swimming and having Saturday brunch for a while. We supported each other. I also made new friends at ProfitLogic. I started hosting wine tasting parties. We started a steak club where we ate different steaks around Boston. Wendy and I started an ABC dining club, eating our way around Boston alphabetically. With my friends, I enjoyed life again and created more positive memories in the real world.

## EMAIL FOR HELP!

It was five years into taking Zyprexa, since my first breakdown, and I was still battling schizophrenia. One day I was at home, and I felt like I was being watched by Joe. I thought I should ask for help because I really didn't know what to do. Compared to my first breakdown, this was nothing. This was just a feeling of someone watching me. Still, I emailed my friends. It was a gut feeling! I sent out an email to about fifteen people:

October 3, 2007 at 10:39 am
Subject: I need help!

Not sure if you remember, and if you have not heard, I had a breakdown a few years ago. Now I seem to be in the same situation again. I am hearing people talking, and my computer "acts" weird. With the combination of hearing what the voices are saying and what's going on around me, it seems I am in trouble, and someone is spying on me and following me around.

I did see a doctor for my breakdown and am taking pills. It seems that it's more than that....

What should I do?

Four friends dropped everything and came to my apartment within fifteen minutes. I was so relieved to see Maggie, Nina, Zoe, and Paige.

"Are you alright?" Maggie said as she walked in. I hugged everyone and started crying. I was so relieved to see them. They all looked very concerned. "What's your doctor's number? Can we go see your doctor?" Maggie continued.

"My doctor?" I was surprised about the question. I gave her his number.

Maggie called the doctor and found out he was on vacation. "We're going to take you to the ER," she said while everyone else stayed quiet.

"Okay." We followed Maggie to her car.

The five of us went to the ER at the New England Medical Center. I was checked in, and we waited in the waiting area. We didn't talk. Everyone looked worried. Nothing was going through my mind. Blank.

Someone at the ER called my name. I was asked to change

into hospital clothing. I didn't know why. I was taken into an examining room. Everyone else had to wait outside. A woman came and asked me a list of questions.

"Do you have thoughts about hurting other people?" the woman asked me.

"No!" *What?*

"Do you have thoughts about hurting yourself?"

"No!" *Why am I being asked this question?*

"Do you have thoughts about killing yourself?"

"No!" I didn't understand what was happening. I was offended.

"Okay. We are done."

I could not believe I was asked these questions and only these questions. It made me feel like I was completely in the wrong place. I was released. My ask-for-help email was covered up and hushed away, as someone explained to everyone else that I was fine.

Maggie and Paige took turns staying with me. I tried to show them I was fine. I acted as if I'd made a mistake asking for help. In the meantime, I was trying to find someone to help me track down the person watching me. I even considered looking for someone professional like a crime detective. But I wasn't one hundred percent sure what was happening, so I didn't look into it seriously. It also didn't occur to me I could go to the police if I thought I would be harmed even though I wasn't yet aware the voices and my hypersensitivity were functions of my brain. None of my friends thought to talk about what I was going through, and I didn't know how to yet. Some of my friends were being respectful of my privacy and didn't ask any questions. Still, they all wanted to be there for me.

Later, when I thought about this, I got mad at myself. *Why didn't I explain myself after everyone got to my apartment? Why did I get so overwhelmed and forget what I was trying to do? Why did I follow Maggie to the ER? What a waste of time!* I found out Maggie was actually acting on a recommendation from a friend's wife who worked with mental patients. She thought that I might be in danger—that I should be sent to an ER as soon as possible before I harmed myself or other people.

I told myself: *Think before you do things. Make sure they make sense. Don't just let friends tell you what to do.* Every time I tried to figure something out, I got interrupted, and it took me awhile to get back on track. I needed to figure out my life for myself. I felt that my friends were making my situation more severe than it actually was. *Don't let them make a big deal out of nothing!*

## WEIGHT AND SLEEP

One day at one of our girls' dinners I explained to my friend Samantha how I was managing. I told her about my wireless scale and sleep tracker. Since I'd started taking medication, I'd experienced fluctuations in my weight and disruptions in my sleep patterns. She said, "Well, at least it's just your weight and sleep. Could be worse."

Although I was a chubby baby, I was a bony teenager. Growing up, I could always eat what I wanted. I loved meat, eggs, and rice. My diet at my childhood home was very simple. When I went to Cornell, I gained the "Freshman Fifteen" because I ate so much new food, especially pasta, cheese, and dessert. That summer I went home and lost all the weight I'd gained during the school year. In my later college years, I went back to my normal eating habits even at school, and once I graduated, I continued to eat whatever I wanted whenever I wanted, without any issues. I bought size 0 and 2 clothing at Banana Republic.

Since I developed schizophrenia and started to take Zyprexa, my body reacted to food differently. The first thing that changed was that I was hungry even after I ate. I'd never felt hungry in my life before, but now I did. I'd never had to resist food, but now my stomach felt like an endless hole. No matter how much food I put into it during a meal, I could always eat more. I loved trying new restaurants with friends. I kept eating and gaining weight. For the second time in my life, I gained weight, another twenty to thirty pounds. I became a size 10 at Banana Republic.

One day I was looking at a picture of Chris and me standing next to each other in my living room. He was slim as usual. I had become double his size. Instead of being a matching pair, my face looked round. My arms were round. My t-shirt fit tightly on my body. After handing me the picture, Chris said, "I don't understand why you don't take care of yourself." I didn't know I had gained so much weight.

I was off my medication a few times when either I'd had a break between prescriptions or was waiting for my next doctor's appointment. I wasn't supposed to have these breaks, but I learned that as soon as I was off Zyprexa, my weight dropped. I would lose fifteen to twenty pounds in a couple of weeks. I would no longer feel hungry. I realized my medication was making me feel hungry. My medication traded one problem for another problem. It's a well-known side effect that Zyprexa causes weight gain. I learned later that sometimes people gain up to hundreds of pounds. Since I still was not aware I had a chronic condition, I was not equipped to manage the condition and the side effects from my medications.

## ANDY AND SUSAN

Since Dan, I had met a few men I liked. Andy was someone I'd met at work. He asked me if I would be interested in going camping with him. I was very comfortable with Andy, so I said yes. We spent one weekend together. It was platonic. Serious dating was the last thing on my mind.

Driving home from Maine, I thought I would open up to him. If he wanted to get to know me better, it was important for him to understand me better.

"So, Andy, there is something I feel like telling you about."

"Oh yeah? What?"

"I had a breakdown a few years ago. I've been going through some stuff..." I hesitated and wanted to see his reaction before I continued. He immediately became quiet. Then he said, "You know what. I know someone who can help you." He took an old-looking business card out of his wallet and handed it to me. "Here. Someone I know. She is very good. You might be able to talk to her."

I kept quiet and didn't say anything more. Andy was one of the first few people I opened up to.

When I got home, I looked at the business card. Susan was a social worker. I'd never talked to a therapist before. I was willing to try. After thinking about it for a few weeks, I called her and made an appointment.

Susan didn't have a separate office, so we met at her house. Coincidentally, she lived on the same street as Chris and I had. I thought it was interesting that Susan brought me back to my old neighborhood. *Is this a good sign?* At the minimum, it was something familiar.

Susan welcomed me into her home. Immediately, I noticed several cats roaming around. She invited me to sit down in her living room. She started the conversations. "Tell me about yourself and your life." I wasn't sure what to say and told her about my grandparents and parents. I didn't have a specific topic in mind for our meetup.

"I want you to think about what you want to do. Write each idea on a sticky. Find a blank wall at home, and put up all the stickies. You can look at this wall everyday and get inspired. This way you won't forget what you want to do."

I was reminded by Susan of all the things I used to like to do. I liked ice skating in the winter when I was a little girl in Taipei. I'd started running when the weather was nice a few years ago. Oh, and I used to go to live performances. I didn't do any of these anymore, but I thought I should start again. In this one session, Susan had put me front and center. She reminded me how to live my life for myself—though I only realized this years later.

I continued to see Susan for about a year. We talked about my life, but I didn't know how to talk about the stuff that was deep inside my head. I stopped seeing her after a while because I felt I could talk about anything I wanted to talk about with my friends. I didn't want to pay money to talk about my everyday life.

## LUPUS AND DAISY

I'd mentioned to Ahmed that I missed Lupus. He suggested that I adopt a cat and took me to Animal Rescue League of Boston. When I saw Daisy, I immediately fell for her. She was a petite female tabby. When I picked her up, she purred. I adopted her that day. Ahmed drove me to a pet store, we picked up everything Daisy needed, and she was home. The shelter guessed she was about two. She'd been picked up off the street and had recently given birth to kittens that had all died. I was happy to bring her into my life. Since I'd helped take care of Lupus, I knew what to do with Daisy. Every day when I came home from work, she greeted me at the door and bunched around next to my feet. Daisy loved playing with strings.

When Chris was out of town for work, he usually left Lupus with me. I divided my apartment into two sections using a baby gate so that Daisy first saw Lupus at a distance. She thought she was the owner of my place. Lupus couldn't care less. He knew he was at my place first. Chris and I were hoping they could keep each other company.

"You can have him. For now," Chris said one day as he was leaving my place. "It would be good if he had a friend."

# 6

# SECOND CHANCE

## Winter 2010

## REDOING IT AGAIN

In 2010, I turned thirty-six, six years after I'd triggered schizophrenia. I was considering becoming a single mother. I thought
that if I wanted to have a family of my own, I should start now
or else it might be too late for me to have a biological child.
Since Chris and I separated, I had not dated anyone else. My
mind was not on dating at all. Becoming a mother on my own
was not an easy choice to make. I talked to as many friends as
I could, got introduced to other single mothers, and found a
local support group for single mothers. I also read books on
other people's experiences with single motherhood and ones
on the opposite experience, of being childless. I still remember
very clearly what one of my good friends told me: "This is your
decision and yours alone. No one can tell you what the best
thing for you to do is. You have to decide." It felt right to me to
try. I wanted to help someone grow up in this world. I wanted
to give to someone.

I finally decided to go ahead with the process of becoming a single mother. I talked to my psychiatrist, Dr. Han. He told me it was okay to stop taking my medication. He didn't explain any risks, but I got the impression the medication might not be something I wanted in my body while I tried. If I noticed anything wrong, he told me, I could always get back on my medication. Not wanting to cause any problems for a potential pregnancy, I stopped taking my medication at the beginning of the summer.

At this time, I was working at a software consulting company called Medullan. I was medication-free without any issue. I focused on becoming pregnant. I was tracking my temperature every day. I was taking vitamins, which I would have never taken before. I shared my process with many girlfriends. Everyone was encouraging.

I had my first IUI, and I was hopeful. I got my period. I was devastated, but I didn't shed any tears. I didn't want to talk to anyone about it. After one try and one failure, I decided I couldn't take the emotional ups and downs of this journey. I decided to stop trying to get pregnant. I started thinking about Joe again. I was remembering the significant and dramatic things that had happened surrounding him. I still had so many questions about what had led to my first mental breakdown. *How had I let myself get to that state?* I replayed everything over and over. I thought about my instincts and reactions, what I didn't do. I cataloged hundreds and thousands of small decisions I'd made. I kept asking myself, *Where was my educated brain? Where was that person who could code complex computer programs and manage expensive software projects?* I looked into getting answers. I decided I wanted a second chance. Maybe I could change the outcome. Maybe I could make it all better. I switched my focus from becoming a single mother and decided to look into my past again.

The first thing I did was go see *Harry Potter* by myself. I hadn't gone to see a movie by myself since my first breakdown. Now I wanted to try again and see what would happen. I thought to myself: *I want to remember why I ended up being so emotional the last time I went to the movies!* Unbelievably, I got my wish. I left the movie halfway through. Words were being whispered next to my right ear. There was loud coughing and laughing. My chair was kicked a few times. It was not quite the same as what I remembered, but it was close enough. It was an ominous feeling that one or more people at the theater were secretly picking on me through orchestrated acts. I had to walk out. When I left the theater, I was so angry. I walked home in the dark. I kept asking myself why this happened to me. *Why am I singled out from the crowd?*

The next night I went back to the same theater to see *Harry Potter* again. I was going to conquer this. This time I sat in the last row, so I could see everyone and everything. I noticed that the man sitting next to me kept looking at me instead of at the screen. He left halfway through the movie, which I didn't care or think much about. I tried to finish the movie and see what else I noticed that was unusual, such as loud coughing to send a signal to me, inconsiderate kicking to purposely distract and upset me, or a quiet whisper next to my ears to tell me something. This time nothing happened, and everything felt normal and as expected. *No one is picking on me!*

*Think! Think! Use your head! It's just a bunch of strangers in a movie theater!* I told myself. If something was annoying or upsetting me, I needed to learn to walk away or change the situation, not just sit there. If someone kicked my seat, I needed to turn around and tell the person to stop. If I felt alone, I needed to ask a friend to come to the movie with me. *Don't just freeze in your seat and be afraid. Don't put yourself in a helpless and fearful position. Don't spend years wondering about this.*

During my second trip to the theater, I didn't hear any whispers. No one was able to kick my seat since I was sitting in the last row. I corrected my automatic thinking. I stopped stringing together a sequence of independent sounds and actions I thought I may have heard or felt while sitting there. I didn't get the feeling that people were trying to communicate with me through unusual means. I started seeing things for what they really were: independent and meaningless occurrences. I felt much, much better.

Now I know, through reading more about schizophrenia, that at some point I'd lost the ability to filter useless information around me. Not only was my mind not filtering out extra information, I made meaning out of the extra information I experienced. This time around, though, I examined my thought process and controlled what I could. I was fighting against the extra synapses in my brain. Regardless of whether that's possible, all that mattered to me was that I felt successful in this do-over.

So, after going to the movie theater, I continued my quest of redoing things. I went on to the next broken memory that had puzzled me every time I thought of it. Because my mind was hypersensitive, it shouldn't have been a surprise that I noticed my surroundings more when I went outside. I felt I was responsible for what I was thinking and how I reacted to people in public. I took whatever small happenings I thought were signals and tried to unlearn my associations with them. Getting signs from strangers was not normal. I needed to reinterpret what I was seeing. This time when I was walking down the street and saw someone touching his ear, I told myself: *It doesn't mean he is telling me to "listen" to him. It's someone touching his ear.*

*That's all.* A car honked. I told myself, *Look at where the sound is coming from. A car is honking at someone crossing the road at a red light. It's not "yes." It's not "right" or "left."* I turned my head, seeing the car hurrying the pedestrians on Newbury Street. The fear of hearing a mystery honk disappeared. I repeated to myself, *Somehow I learned this was magical. Now I need to unlearn that.* Perhaps, in a movie, a stranger can leave secret messages for a woman, like in *Amélie.* Or a little girl can follow a rabbit down a hole in the ground to a magical world, like in *Alice in Wonderland.* But Amélie and young Alice are both fictional characters. In real life, there are situations where people do signal to each other. For example, during a baseball game, the coach signals to his team. But no one talks in signals with strangers in real life. If I followed someone I didn't know into a restaurant because I saw him look at me invitingly that would be considered strange or even dangerous. Even if some people do communicate with unspoken hints, I wanted them to talk to me directly at this point. I was fixing another problem based on changing my behavior and my way of thinking. I went on to my next problem.

I hadn't listened to music as much as I had before my breakdown. I might've been avoiding it even though I'd wanted songs to be an important part of my life. I decided to use an online music app called Spotify. I wanted to see how I would react to music.

When I heard a phrase that sparked emotion in me, I thought how it was okay I liked a phrase in a song. I could feel amazed by how coincidental it was to like a lyric from a song and hear the song played on the radio, remembering there was no one playing the songs just for me. *I happen to listen and like mainstream music. I am not that original when it comes to liking songs. I like songs that everyone likes.* The computer was playing songs for me and everyone else in the world.

I felt better again. I was correcting more mistakes I had made. I was doing-over the most puzzling experiences in my adult life. *What's next?*

## KEEPING IN TOUCH

I had no intention of unearthing my past alone. The last time I hadn't shared what I was going through, I'd had a major breakdown. I couldn't speak at the end of it at all. I was knocked out by medication for days. I was lucky I woke up my old self again.

I thought to tell someone what I was doing. I called my friend Samantha and asked her to meet me for a sushi lunch in Davis Square. I decided to open up completely. I thought about what I was facing and tried to explain to her what I was thinking. It was hard to explain everything, but I had to start somewhere.

"I want to tell you what I'm up to, but it's hard to explain. It might sound a little odd or crazy!" I told Samantha.

"Okay." She smiled and encouraged me to go on.

I explained to her that what I wanted to do might be a combination of different things. I was still trying to figure out how to solve my own problems. I felt that a doctor might solve them one way while a detective would solve them another way. For example, the doctor would check to see if my body was healthy and, if not, might prescribe medication. A detective could look into someone signaling to me or following me around. It's not that I was thinking I should hire a detective; I just wanted someone who could act like a detective and help me figure things out, I told her. I tried to explain all of this delicately since I didn't want Samantha to be alarmed.

"I'm not taking my medication," I said slowly.

"Oh. You may want to work with a doctor if you want to get off your medication. You should phase that out. Don't just stop. There are very specific ways of doing it."

"I've been off medication for a few months actually. I talked to my doctor about it before I stopped." I went on to tell her my conversation with my doctor and the reason I stopped.

Then I told her a few examples of what had been bothering me that week. I told her I noticed my surroundings a bit more, such as gestures from strangers as I walked by them or at the movies. I wanted to see if I could still notice anything unusual. This time I didn't summarize and make conclusions. I didn't think and say there might be someone organizing all of these happenings just for me. I didn't jump to the conclusion that someone was sending me special messages. I told her specifics, sticking to what I thought were facts.

"I just want to let someone know what I'm doing. Just in case," I said at the end.

"Okay." She did not react negatively to my talk with her.

This was the beginning of my opening up to friends with more specifics. Samantha and many of my friends stood by me as I worked through my thoughts. What I valued most was—and is—that they listened, reasoned with me, and challenged me. They did not treat me any differently from the old me. I was the same person they knew, and I was still a functional, responsible, and independent person from what they could see. I was still living my life.

A few weeks later, after my conversation with Samantha, I woke up one night at two in the morning, crying again. I was not sad. I didn't know why I burst out crying in the middle of the night while I was sleeping. Even though I thought I was in control of things, it seemed my body was reacting to my do-over negatively in some way. I wanted to get help right there, right then in the middle of my cry. The first person I thought to call was Maggie. I dialed her number without a second thought.

"Hi," I managed to say, crying uncontrollably when she answered the phone.

"Hi. Are you okay?? Do you want me to come over? What's wrong?" Maggie said anxiously.

"No. I'm fine." I felt a bit better already.

"Are you sure?"

"Yes." I stopped crying.

"Are you sure?" Maggie asked again.

"Yeah. I'm fine. Sorry I'm calling in the middle of the night."

"It's okay."

"I'm fine. Thanks! Good night."

"Okay. Good night," Maggie said.

After we hung up, she told me later she'd worried about me the whole night. She couldn't get back to sleep. I'm sure her imagination told me I was in trouble again. She probably thought of me getting hurt. She took the next day off from work and came over to my place in the morning. I was not expecting to see her. We were calm and pleasant to each other, no different from how we usually met each other. She said we should go and see my doctor, Dr. Han. I didn't understand why I should talk to my psychiatrist, but I followed her lead because I also felt something was not quite right. Part of me wanted to see if she had any idea what might help me. But I was not thinking for myself again.

On the way to the hospital, I asked her about something I had experienced a few days earlier.

"I heard you talking to me!" I said. I smiled and hoped to find out more. I wondered what she thought of it.

"Really?" Maggie said while driving, looking straight at the road in front of the car. She smiled too. She didn't say anything else.

"Yes. You asked me to call you." I didn't want to give up on this conversation. I smiled and said a bit more.

"Really?" Smiled. Silence again.

Me: "Yeah."

There was silence. She didn't know what else to say. I didn't know what else to say either. We didn't talk for the rest of the way. When we got to the hospital, Maggie was able to get an emergency appointment. We walked into Dr. Han's messy, small office together. We sat across from Dr. Han as I'd done alone many times before. Maggie spoke right away. She told him she was a friend of mine and that I had been very upset the night before.

"Okay," he said, unmoved and with no emotion.

"She is not taking her medication," Maggie said, stressed by her worry.

"If she's not taking her medication, there is nothing I can do for her," Dr. Han said. Maggie was surprised and upset. How could he not help? "I can't make her take her medication," he continued.

"But you have to help her."

"There is nothing I can do for her if she does not listen to me. I told her already. If she takes her medication, everything will be fine."

I didn't say anything. I didn't mention how I had been trying to get pregnant. I just sat there and watched them get into an argument. It felt like their conversation had little to do with me. At the end, Maggie and I just left the doctor's office. While we walked down the hallway, she figured out what she wanted me to do next. "You have to go to the ER," she said.

"No, I am not going to the ER. I don't need to go to the ER." I didn't know what she was thinking. I felt fine.

"You have to either take your pill now or go to the ER."

"No, I'm going home. This is ridiculous." I had been to the ER once. I knew what it was for. It was for people who were thinking about either hurting other people or hurting themselves. The ER was for emergencies. I left Maggie and walked out of the hospital. I thought to myself, *So I cried last night. So what? I never should have called her.* I took the T and went straight home.

Shortly after I arrived, someone came knocking very loudly on my door.

"Hello! Hello. Anyone home?" a man said.

I opened the door. Two men in uniforms stood in front of me.

"How are you?" The second man said.

"Good."

"There was a report that someone ran away from the hospital. Is everything okay? Are you alone?" *I did not run away from the hospital. I left on my own will.*

"Yes. I'm alone. I'm fine."

"Do you need any help?"

"No. I'm fine. "

Maggie arrived at my apartment and stood behind the men. She was crying.

"Okay. If you need anything, let us know."

Everyone turned away from the door and left. I closed the door behind them. I couldn't believe Maggie had told them I ran away. *Why did she say that?* I had never had an EMT or anyone else chasing after me. It felt like they thought I'd done something wrong. I was really mad at Maggie. *She doesn't think I have a brain*, I thought. She was not making it easier for me. She was adding more stress and confusion when I was already dealing with reexamining and correcting my own thinking and behaviors. I didn't understand what she was thinking. She was involving more people who did not understand me and what I had been going through alone. Many years later, I would understand her perspective better: no one knew exactly what the best thing was for me. Everyone, including Maggie, was just doing what they thought was right. Everyone was guessing and doing their best.

A few hours later, after I calmed down, I got a call from Samantha. She and Paige wanted to come over to see me that night. I was not expecting visitors on such short notice and was surprised. But they were close friends, and I said okay. Samantha and Paige brought dinner when they came. I started talking to them about my day and explained what had happened. I didn't know it, but Maggie had already talked to my friends, including Samantha and Paige even though I had never introduced her to them before. Now I can't help but see the irony in what my friends were trying to do. If I had been a bit more paranoid, having my friends from different groups coming together behind my back might have freaked me out. While Samantha, Paige, and I sat in my living room, I talked about what I could do as I tried very hard to explain to them what I was thinking. We were able to agree that waking up crying in the middle of the night was not a good thing. They suggested I see another doctor. I was okay with that. "Perhaps your primary care doctor?" Paige asked. I trusted her. "Let's give her a call tomorrow and tell her about it."

"Okay."

"Do you want me to come with you?"

"Yes."

"Okay, I will." We all had the same doctor and liked being under her care.

The next day Samantha took off from work and went with me to Massachusetts General Hospital (MGH). While we were waiting to see my doctor, Samantha handed me a pamphlet on schizophrenia. I didn't read it and put it in my bag. When I was called, I asked Samantha to stay with me while I talked to our doctor. The three of us crowded in the small examining room. This was the first time I talked in detail about what I'd been imagining to someone out loud. "I first got sick around when I was thirty." I started from the beginning. I told my primary care doctor about Joe. I told her about what I was trying to do now by giving myself a second chance. I told her I thought people had been signaling to me—how I felt people might be able to read my mind and poke me.

"I highly recommend you talk to a psychiatrist," my doctor said.

I explained myself a bit more.

"I highly recommended you talk to a psychiatrist," the doctor said again.

"Okay, I'll remember that."

Both my doctor and Samantha were extremely worried. I told myself not to ignore their worries. I respected their opinions. I should be careful, but I was not worried myself. I knew how it felt before I had my breakdown. And I was feeling fine. My head was okay still. My primary care doctor gave me a number to call. I promised I would call the psychiatry department. I wanted to get the right person to help me.

When I got home, I looked at the pamphlet Samantha had given me. I realized some of the ways I described my experiences were similar to what was outlined in the pamphlet. I made a mental note of this too. *I should remember this and be careful about how I describe my experience as not to mislead people.*

I also gave her Dr. Han's (my primary care doctor) contact information since she had asked if I was seeing a psychiatrist and if it was okay to speak to him. I didn't see any harm and signed the consent. She tried unsuccessfully to contact Dr. Han. She got a message saying he was ramping down his practice and was out of reach, so she couldn't get access to my earlier medical records or get his opinion about my current situation. At this point, it was clear to my doctor I did not have a psychiatrist who was talking to and helping me. She also had to rely on my recollection of what medications I tried and when, and I wasn't able to tell her specifics. Since my experience wasn't her specialty, all she could do was refer me to someone she trusted.

During this time, Samantha was in touch with Maggie. They disagreed on how they should help me. Maggie wanted to do things for me. For example, she wanted someone to make me take my medication, so I could be fixed right away. Samantha believed I needed to work out my situation on my own and at my own pace. "No one can force Mindy to do anything she doesn't want to do." It was tough for me, and it was tough for all my friends who cared about me.

I did think about getting more professional help while I was working out my own way to a solution. I remembered how I'd asked my primary care doctor to recommend a therapist. I wanted to try someone different than Susan, with a different style, maybe someone who would have a way to fix my problem without using medication. I took out the list my doctor had given me. I looked up all five therapists. They had different focuses, such as life coaching, crisis management, depression, weight management. I finally settled on Mary, who focused on life coaching. I thought the problems I was facing could fall under that category. I called her and made an appointment.

I saw Mary a few times. She had a beautiful office in Back Bay, which looked like something out of an interior design magazine, and she dressed very well like someone out of a fashion magazine. For instance, she wore a two-piece suit to our sessions. During our first meeting, she did an intake interview. I should have known she was not the therapist I was looking for by her first question: "What kind of beverage do you like to order when you go out with friends to a bar?" Her focus was around my ability to be social and make friends. She asked about my parents, my childhood, and my current situation. I didn't hold back. I changed the subject and told her everything I was going through, including my earlier breakdown. She seemed a little taken aback. This was not her expertise, but she tried to help me. She let me do most of the talking. Her practice didn't accept my insurance, so the session cost me 300 dollars. After seeing her three times, I decided I was not getting the help I needed, plus it was expensive. Mary also asked me for consent, so she could contact my doctor, which she did.

I also called Susan again. This time I told Susan the deeper issues I was facing. She told me she knew a psychiatrist who was very knowledgeable. He believed in the plasticity of the mind and could potentially help me through psychotherapy, which sounded good to me. Perhaps he would not just tell me to take a pill. I asked Susan to make an introduction. She wrote an email to the psychotherapist, cc'ing me:

Hi XX, I would like to refer Mindy to you. She is hearing voices, but managing it. However, the intrusive nature of them is really getting in her way. She has been on Zyprexa, which helped, but she is seeking a consultation and hopefully you can get her squared away with psychotropic medications. There is a history of paranoid schizophrenia in the family (namely, her mom). Thanks so much.

The word that stuck in my head was "schizophrenia." I hadn't wanted her to mention that. I wanted the doctor to hear my side of the story before making a judgment. I hadn't concluded I had schizophrenia and didn't want someone to label me. I was in the middle of investigating it. Regardless, I would see this doctor and see if he could help me. I had a plan with three options: see the doctor Susan referred me to, call the psychiatric department at MGH, which my primary care doctor had referred me to, or go back and see Dr. Han. I wanted a few days to think things over.

## VOICES AGAIN

After this, I started hearing voices again.

When I'd first heard Joe, I imagined a young man talking into a microphone in a room somewhere. Somehow I could hear him through some impressive technology I was not aware of. He was soft spoken, friendly, and not terribly talkative. Mostly, he made comments about what I did. He was not particularly funny or smart. I couldn't tell if he was logical because we didn't have enough "conversations" that would make me think that. I couldn't get him to tell me anything about himself. We took turns "talking" and never talked over each other. He never yelled or whispered.

Once in a while, he would tell me what to do, but they were harmless actions. Still, I tried to reason with him. I thought if I could figure out what he wanted, then I might be able to get rid of him or get him to show up. As described earlier, I wasn't successful. Then I became romantic. I developed a little crush on Joe. I thought I was being helped by him magically. But I kept repeatedly facing the reality of the nonexistence of a real boy.

The next time I heard voices, I didn't hear just one voice but many different voices. The other voices were of people I knew: friends and family. These voices took me right back to a world of my own alone in my apartment. They led me to have personal conversations and play fun games. I tried to fight against these voices, but I was often consumed and swallowed by them completely.

When I first heard my family, I felt disbelief. *This cannot be my grandmother, could it? She would not talk to me this way. She wouldn't put me through this.* But my disbelief did not stop the voices. Different circles of friends talked to me on different days. I made rules for myself concerning how I should behave: *don't do anything they tell me to do. Don't talk back to them using my mouth.* Following my rules, I thought, would mean I was okay. Okay in terms of what, I wasn't sure, but it seemed to make sense then. I tried to be logical, reasonable, and understanding with them, but that did not seem to matter to the voices of my friends and family.

I tried to understand how these voices worked. I knew the difference between the voices and people actually talking even though I "heard" both. When someone talked, I heard the words in my head one way. The voices sounded like talking that I heard with my ears, except that the talking came from different spots near me. In other words, the voices appeared out of thin air. Even though I knew the difference, I instinctively imagined and believed a real person was behind each voice. I just couldn't see the person. To make it more complicated, there were other nonverbal sounds, such as raindrops, birds, my laptop, and all these sounds were saying something to me.

I moved around in the apartment and realized the voices did not move with me. If I turned my head to look out the window, the voices I "heard" changed how they should. In other words, when I walked out of my apartment, the talking sounds stayed in my living room at the far end of the hallway. I used earplugs to block off the voices when I tried to fall asleep. The earplugs helped. Similarly, I could block out the voices by listening to music on headphones. When I was out of the house and among people, the voices traveled with me but were less prominent. They became background noise. Unless I focused on them, they did not interfere with what I was doing.

Even though I figured out ways to block out the voices, I couldn't do it for long. For instance, I couldn't wear earplugs or listen to music all day. I ended up hearing the voices most of the time and giving them my attention. But I never thought I was the cause of the voices.

I wasn't watching TV or using the computer outside of work while I was experiencing these symptoms. Because of this, I had eliminated a lot of external stimuli that could create more problems for me. For example, I would not see people on TV gesturing strangely and possibly sending me messages. I wouldn't see the computer mouse moving slightly without my hand touching the mouse. I reached out to more friends. I started asking more questions. Every time I asked a question, I was using all of the courage I had in me.

One of the people whom I asked directly was Ryan. I met Ryan at Medullan. He and his wife were both from Vermont and had become my good friends beyond working together. Ryan was personable and considerate. I could ask him anything. One night Ryan and his wife came over to my place to get ready for a party. My mind was only half on the party. Before the three of us left for our apartment, I said, "Can I ask you something?" Ryan was always helpful and a good friend.

"Of course!"

I sat down on my sofa, and he pulled a chair to sit in front of me. "You know, I heard you all morning," I said lightly to Ryan.

"Really?" He smiled. He did not look surprised. It was as if we were talking about something normal. He gave me an encouraging look to keep talking.

I thought, *Don't you think that's weird?* But Ryan didn't respond. I felt awkward. I quickly changed the subject. "Are we ready to leave?" During the party, I tried to focus on what was happening. I definitely felt mentally tired and was thankful Ryan was there to take some attention away from me.

That Saturday my college friend Levina called me to ask how I was doing. I wasn't in the habit of talking to friends on the phone. I was surprised to get a call from her. After talking for a bit about how I was, I felt brave and approached the subject of the voices. "I heard you chanting this morning!" I said, recalling how her chanting had reminded me of monks in a Buddhist temple.

"Really? What did I say?" We were on the phone, so I couldn't see her expression, but she sounded upbeat like her usual self.

*Now what do I say?* I thought. "I don't know. I couldn't really hear what you were saying. You were just talking really fast."

Again, I didn't know how to bring up the questions in my mind and quickly changed the subject because it seemed she didn't know what I was talking about. I wasn't able to get any answers from her because I didn't know how to ask her a clear question.

On another day late in the night I heard a group of friends having a party in my living room for a few hours. I was fed up. I picked up the phone and called one of them, Andy. "Sorry to call so late. Can I ask you a question? I heard you talking to me. Were you just talking to me a few minutes ago?"

"No," Andy said quickly. There was silence for a few seconds as if both of us were searching for the right words to say next.

"Is Lani there?" Lani was Andy's wife and also a good friend.

"Yes, I am here," she said quickly.

"You didn't talk to me before this?" I asked again, wanting to make sure.

"No. Are you okay?" Andy and Lani said at the same time. They sounded concerned. I had never called them so late. We hadn't talked in awhile.

"Okay. I should go." I didn't want to explain what I was going through. There was too much to explain.

"Are you okay? Do you want to talk about it?" Andy asked.

"Sorry to call so late. I've got to go. Bye!" I had gotten my answer. If they understood what was going on, they didn't want to tell me.

After I hung up with Andy and Lani, I tried to figure out what to do next. I could ask someone to check out the party noise happening upstairs from my apartment. I called the local police. A woman answered. "I think I hear my friends upstairs. Can you check it out?"

"Are they causing you problems?"

"I can hear talking from upstairs."

"Do they live upstairs?"

"No, they don't."

"It doesn't sound like there is a problem."

"Okay. Thanks," I said and hung up the phone, feeling stuck again.

Out of the blue, a few days after I called my friends, my dad called me and asked if he could come over. When he called, he was in the car with my stepmother and stepbrother.

Around the time I'd graduated from college, Dad and Mother had separated. I'd always felt they were incompatible and was very happy for them to make the change. Dad stayed in New Jersey, and Mother moved to New York. Mother claimed she didn't need a man in her life. Since her first and only hospitalization when Oliver and I dropped her off at the ER in NYC, Mother had been on medication and, as far as I knew, had never had another episode. I believed she was now happily living a single life, working full-time as an accountant, and playing Taiwanese mahjong with neighbors on weekends. On the other hand, Dad had met another woman, who had a son eight years younger than me, and he enjoyed having another woman in his life. I was happy for him.

Dad and my stepmother lived five hours away from me. They only visited during my major life events, such as moving to Boston from college and buying my first apartment. I could count them on one hand. Since college, I had been living a very independent life.

"Why do you want to come over all of a sudden on a Wednesday?" I asked Dad, since he had always been very committed to his work. He never took days off from work unless it was an emergency.

"Oh nothing. I just thought maybe I should come over and see you. I'm actually already on my way."

"Why? What's wrong?" I asked, getting a little upset. I could tell he was worried, but I didn't know why.

"Nothing. Nothing. If you are fine, then that's good," he said.

"Yes, I'm fine. There's no need for you to come over. It's a weekday. I have stuff to do. I can't spend time with you if you come. We can plan on an upcoming weekend if you want to come and visit," I said, still trying to understand why my dad was acting so strange.

After the phone call, I thought, *What the heck?* Something was up. I was mad. I had to stop whatever he planned to do. I didn't need one more problem in my life.

Later, I found out Maggie had called my parents. It felt like someone had sent out a memo about me. It was frustrating enough trying to figure out what was wrong with me; I now had more people whose feelings about me I had to manage. I wanted to say to my parents and friends: "Why do you believe other people more than me? Next time, come and ask me if you hear something. Check with me first! Ask! Ask me!"

Later on, I found out *all* of my friends were in touch with each other by this time. Andy had called Maggie after my strange phone call at midnight. They were all trying to figure out how to help me, and everyone had different opinions. While I was trying to solve my own problems, everyone was trying to solve me.

Chris was in Hong Kong at the time. Because he was away, I was able to handle the situation my own way. No one dropped by unannounced. No one came and yelled at me. No one pulled me out of my world. So I stayed with the voices of my friends and family.

Early the next morning, I got a text from Ahmed who was also now the CEO at Medullan, the company where I was working. "Do you want to meet for breakfast?"

"Yes. Let's do that," I texted back.

We met in front of my apartment building and walked over to Trident Cafe on Newbury Street. I think he asked me how I was. I might have said I was dealing with a few things. I was being careful. I didn't want to freak him out with specific details. I didn't want to talk about anything I hadn't quite figured out yet.

At one point, while I was talking, I hesitated and looked to the right. There was a woman sitting next to our table. "Why don't we pack our food to go? And talk in your apartment? More privacy that way?" Ahmed said. I didn't care about the woman, but going to my place to talk was okay by me.

On the way back to my apartment, we continued our chat. When we were almost back to my apartment, I started really crying. Ahmed hugged me, and I tried to pull myself back together. We sat in my apartment, and he asked me what I was thinking. He was one of the very few people who asked in that way.

"The situation I'm in is hard to explain." I looked around my apartment and saw the TV cabinet. "For example, if you look at the different parts that go into making the TV work, there are plugs in the wall, wires, and the TV itself. If the TV doesn't work properly, then it could be any part that's broken. It could also be the signals coming from the network company."

He continued to talk to me for almost the whole day even though I probably didn't make much sense. I didn't really know how to talk about my experience yet, but I tried my best. Around three that afternoon, he looked at his watch and reluctantly said, "There's nothing I can do for you, unfortunately. And now I gotta go."

"Thanks for coming and checking up on me," I said meaningfully. It was great knowing I could talk to a friend openly, who wouldn't freak out on me. He also didn't do anything to scare me. He didn't call someone to drag me away. At this time, I was more frustrated with most of my real friends and family than with their imaginary voices.

At this time, I still believed the voices were from real people. I thought my friends and family could read my mind and speak to me telepathically. So I felt that I didn't have any privacy, not even in my mind, because I couldn't shut the voices off.

Unlike the first time when I went through living with a voice, I was not afraid of my own mind this time. I didn't hesitate to think. I didn't feel embarrassed about my thoughts even if they were crazy. Now I believe I had the initial breakdown because I was trying to hide from my own thoughts. *Be confident about what I think. Every thought. Don't be embarrassed*, I told myself.

One day on the way to work, I thought up a story to describe my situation. Hearing a voice and now hearing voices again were like two separate marriages. During my first marriage, the guy mistreated me over and over again. I could not leave him. But my friends helped me get away. During my second marriage, the second husband mistreated and abused me too, caused me pain, but this time, even though I was more aware of the situation, I still wasn't able to leave, and even my friends couldn't help me. I lived in agony with no way out.

My frustration had been building up little by little over the past three months. One afternoon during a work day, I was sitting on my queen-sized bed not knowing what to do. I'd taken a shower and dressed myself after waking up. I hadn't eaten anything. I'd been home all day. By this time, the days started to blur, and voices became a constant. My focus was becoming more and more inward on the voices, but they still felt like real people I was listening to. I looked out my window and saw bright sunlight. It must have been a beautiful day outside. I tried to do something productive again, like when I'd gone to see *Harry Potter*. I opened my laptop and stared at the screen unable to focus. *Should I unfriend everyone on Facebook, so I can be sure no one knows what I am up to and isolate my problem?* I felt suspicious of social media. Then I realized, *It would be silly to isolate myself that way!* Removing friends online wouldn't really help my situation. I closed the laptop and opened it again minutes after. *What should I do now?* I was running out of creative ideas. *Bang. Bang.* Someone knocked loudly on my door. I hurried to open the door and saw two EMTs standing in front of me. Both of them smiled, and one of them said, "We got a call. We're looking for a teenage girl. Can we come in?" I let them in while trying to prevent my two cats from getting out. I didn't know the teenage girl they were looking for. By now, I was no longer surprised by EMT visits. The three of us stood in my hallway.

"How are you?" the tall one asked.

"I'm fine. Thanks," I said.

"Are you here by yourself?"

"Yes."

"How is everything? Do you need help?" the tall one asked.

"Maybe. Yes, I think I need help," I said.

"Do you want to come with us?" the tall one smiled.

I thought for a few seconds and said, "Yeah, I think so. Okay."

I started to put on my shoes and jacket. My cats Lupy and Daisy noticed the visitors and came over and started rubbing my legs. "You have two cats," the shorter man commented.

"Yeah. They are great! I should make sure they have enough food and water before I go," I said.

"I have a dog. I can show you a picture," the short man said, showing me a picture from his wallet, which distracted me, so I forgot all about going to check on food and water for my cats.

The EMTs had come at the right time. I was ready to do something else. *Anything!* I grabbed my bag with my wallet, phone, and keys, locked my door, and the three of us left my apartment. *I give up!* I thought. *If you think you can help me, please go ahead because I don't know what else to do!* I got into their ambulance. I remember how big the back of it felt. It swallowed me up. I didn't talk to the EMT who sat there with me. He asked for my identification and some general information, so I handed him my driver's license. Or maybe it was the insurance card. I didn't know how they'd landed at my home. I didn't know who had called them. I cried immediately after I got into the ambulance, letting out of all of my frustration at the end of this three-month period.

Later on, I found out Maggie had called the EMT on me again because a few days before we'd talked briefly on the phone. I don't remember that conversation at all.

It was a short ride from my apartment to MGH. The tall guy escorted me straight through the ER. A few more nurses surveyed me and passed me farther and farther into the building. I was told to change into hospital clothing. I was told to wait in a small room by myself. I was getting upset. I really wanted someone to understand how I felt having been "talked to" when I was alone for the past three months. How I had tried to listen but couldn't figure out what it all meant.

While waiting in the small room by myself, I called my friends one by one, connecting them by merging the calls one after another until I had ten of them. I didn't say a word to anyone on this call. New voices just showed up on the line. I thought, *See how confusing it is? Can you understand?*

Eventually, after a few minutes, I hung up. My friend Samantha showed up at the ER not too long after. When she saw me, she asked, "How are you?" When I saw her, I burst out crying. Then she hugged me tightly. She stayed with me in the tiny room until around midnight when I was called to see one more doctor. I went to another room that was bigger than the waiting room I'd been sitting in. Samantha was asked to wait outside. My cousin Chao also came but wasn't allowed in at all. He was told I was only allowed one visitor at a time. Then they were both told I couldn't have any more visitors for the night.

The doctor asked me questions, and I nodded my head, shook my head, or gave short replies. Once that was done, someone, a nurse probably, came and asked me to take something. He told me it was orange juice and vitamins. I took the pills and went to sleep on a couch in that room. I realized how so very tired I was when I finally let go. I went into a deep sleep.

# 7

# LOCKED UP

## February 2011

### MEDICAL RECORD: ADMISSION NOTES 02/09/11

After falling asleep at the ER, I don't have any memory of what happened during the following twelve-hour period. However, I was able to get a copy of my hospital records, and this is what the attending physician wrote, mostly based on my responses to his questions at the Acute Psychiatry Service (APS) at MGH. The report also seems to include additional details from my friends.

Chief complaint: This is a thirty-seven-year-old, Asian-American female with a history of schizophrenia, with no previous hospitalizations, and no significant past medical history, who was brought in by EMS after the patient's friend called 911 for increasing psychotic symptoms in the context of stopping her Zyprexa.

Mental status examination on admission: The patient is a thin, Asian-American woman in hospital attire. She is sedated and minimally responsive to verbal stimuli. She will nod "yes" or "no" to safety questions, but she refuses to answer further. No speech is observed. Her mood, thought process, and thought content are unable to be assessed. Thought content likely is significant for an underlying psychotic process, and this interviewer questions if some of what appear to be sedation are underlying psychotic symptoms. Insight and judgement is limited by sedation at this time. Attention, orientation, and memory were unable to be assessed secondary to the patient's sedation.

Inventory of assets: The patient is reported to be bright and articulate with good social and family support.

Formulation: This is a thirty-seven-year-old female with a history of schizophrenia currently decompensated with increased psychotic symptoms in the setting of stopping Zyprexa with hopes to conceive a child. Her family and friends are concerned about her safety and recent erratic behavior and brought her to medical attention. In the APS, she was given 5 mg of oral Zyprexa and is currently sedated in the CEC (Clinical Evaluation Center at McLean) and unable to participate in the interview in a meaningful way. This lack of participation may also be representative of her underlying psychotic process. She requires an inpatient level of care for safety, stabilization, medication re-initiation and management, diagnostic clarification, and aftercare planning.

Initial treatment plan: To admit the patient to AB2. Estimated length of stay of seven to ten days. We will put her on fifteen-minute checks while restricted. Initial short-term goals are safety and stabilization. Recommended interventions include individual case management, group therapy, milieu therapy, pharmacotherapy, family meeting, medication management, and psychosocial interventions.

## MCLEAN IN-PATIENT AB2 UNIT

As soon as I woke up, I jumped out of bed and looked around. I didn't recognize where I was. Furniture was the only thing in the room. There were two other twin beds, three wooden desks with chairs next to them, and the walls were bare. There was only one door to go in and out. I heard nothing. My mind was clear. There were no thoughts running through it.

I saw two brown paper bags on the desk next to my bed. They were the kind of brown paper bags from grocery stores. In them, I found my clothes and handbag. I looked down at myself. I was wearing a brown cotton shirt and pants. They were not mine. I immediately picked up my handbag and checked my things. *Is everything here? No! My iPhone is gone. My wallet is gone, but my house keys are here.* There was a small plastic cup filled with quarters in my handbag. The cup looked liked hospital urine cups for taking tests. My heart skipped a beat. I didn't panic, but I felt something was terribly wrong.

I remembered I had been in a deep sleep, where I vaguely felt someone put a needle into my left arm. The needle hadn't woken me completely. I remembered hands putting a bandage where the needle was. My mind had felt very heavy. I fell back to sleep. It happened again. I heard a man next to me talk about drawing blood. This time I mumbled *no* with my eyes closed. My right hand moved to cover my left arm. He didn't draw any more blood from me. My mind still felt heavy. I fell back to sleep again. Someone came again. I heard a cart rolling toward me. Something was taped on my head and body. Someone was measuring my heartbeat, I thought. Even with all that, I didn't wake up. I fell back to sleep again. I didn't know how long I slept. *Did all that happen while I was on this bed in this room?* I didn't know.

I took my own familiar clothes out of one of the two brown paper bags on the desk. I quickly put on my dark brown sweater, blue jeans, light brown wool coat, and white knitted scarf. There was comfort in putting on and wearing my own clothes. I felt I'd gained back some control and order in the few minutes where I put on my own clothes. I grabbed my brown handbag and walked out of the room. "I am leaving!" I mumbled to myself and made up my mind.

Walking out of the room, I turned right. I talked to the first person I met in the hallway. He was a thin white man with short hair wearing regular clothes. He was standing in the middle of the hallway, reading something on a clipboard in his hand.

"I want to leave," I said to the stranger, urgently focused on my only thought at the moment.

"You can't," he said.

I reacted. "Look, there is a urine cup in my bag. My wallet and phone are missing. Why is there a urine cup with coins in my bag?" I said louder than I normally speak. I wanted answers.

"I don't know," he said sympathetically and calmly in a matter-of-fact way. I wondered if he'd been in this kind of situation a thousand times before me. I looked at him; he looked at me. Silence filled the next few seconds. It was not in my nature to be confrontational or argumentative. The stranger obviously wasn't trying to help me. He just looked at me gently. Neither of us moved. I didn't think of asking where I was, or why, even though he probably knew more about my situation than I did. I turned away from him. He didn't come after me.

I walked back to the room, still agitated from talking loudly, still wanting to leave. I looked out the window to see if I could tell where I was. I saw a garden with many trees and snow on the ground. There was no one outside. I could tell I wasn't in Boston anymore. There weren't any packed brownstone buildings, narrow streets, or endless cars and pedestrians. It actually looked peaceful and spacious outside. I noticed the windows were sealed and locked with metal bars. I noticed a piece of paper on the desk. I didn't really read it, but I spotted the word *Belmont*.

*Okay, Belmont,* I thought, still focused on leaving this room that was not mine. *As long as I have my keys, I can still go home. I can walk home to Back Bay from Belmont. I've done that before for the three-day breast cancer walk. It might take me all day, but I can do it!* I quickly estimated the number of hours it would take in my head. I knew Belmont was a town about eight miles from Boston. Without any money or a phone, I thought I could get to somewhere familiar. I thought, *I have my legs. I can depend on myself. I can figure this out!* I wasn't worried. If I put my mind to it, I could fix my situation, whatever it was. I snuck out of the room more quietly this time. I turned left, heading towards the longer side of the hallway and looked for an exit door. I didn't see anything obvious. I didn't run into anyone this time. All of a sudden, in the quiet hallway, I felt like I was doing something wrong by trying to leave. Plus, I couldn't find an easy way out. Looking for an exit door and being stuck in this hallway made me anxious. My actions felt useless. After a few more minutes, I changed my mind. I stopped trying to leave and decided to go back to the room. I took off my jacket, put down my handbag, and sat down on the bed. This time I gave my mind some space to wander. I noticed sunlight coming through the windows. There were three windows along the wall opposite the door. Besides the brightness, the room was very clean and simple and reminded me of my college dorm when I'd first moved in. I remembered how that room had felt, as if the room itself was eagerly waiting for someone to live in it. The urgency to leave and the feeling of strangeness went away. I've always been good at being flexible and making sense of the unexpected.

From my surroundings and what the thin white man had said, I somehow realized I was now locked up. I didn't need to talk to anyone to understand this. What I didn't know was how I had gotten here. The last thing I remembered was when I was at the ER. It was late at night, probably close to midnight. I remembered someone asking me questions. He wore a white coat and might have been a doctor. After he'd finished with his questions, I was tired and fell asleep on a sofa. The talking— that must have been an evaluation. After that, a doctor at the ER must have admitted me to this place. *Was it overnight?* I didn't remember any of the questions or what I had said. *Did I not make any sense? Did I say something wrong?* I noticed two plastic bracelets around my wrist. The white one had my name, birthday, and gender on it. The blue one also had my name and birthday plus "Admit 02/09/11." I didn't know what date it was. *I'm in a hospital.*

I saw the green piece of paper on the desk again. On the top it said, "Welcome to ABII." In clear black letters, it also said:

The Focus of ABII
AB II is a locked, teaching inpatient unit that cares for adults with psychotic disorders, including schizophrenia, bipolar illness, major depression, delusional disorders, severe compulsive disorders, and other related disorders of thinking, mood, and behavior. A treatment team will work with you and your family to provide assessment and intervention in the areas of diagnosis, medication management, treatment planning, patient and family education, and discharge planning.

There was more information, but I stopped reading. A map was on a second piece of white paper. I saw the name *McLean Hospital.* I assumed it was a map of the facility. It looked like a plus sign. In the middle of the sign, it said *Nurse Station.* The four arms were the *North, East, South,* and *West* wings. I stopped looking again. At the age of thirty-seven, I was suddenly confined at an inpatient restricted unit for the first time in my life. *How did I get here? What had happened? What did I do?* Sometime later, I would receive a bill from an ambulance company for the non-emergency ride from MGH to McLean for $258.72. I felt something was amiss. I was a Cornell-educated woman who had a steady job, lived independently for all of her adult life, traveled the world, and had loving friends and family. I tried to retrace my steps. I started going over it again in my head.

I realized this situation had simplified my life: I couldn't work. I didn't have my laptop, my phone, or my books. I couldn't go anywhere. My basic needs were taken care of. I had a place to sleep. I had food to eat. I felt safe. No strangers could come in. I was free of any responsibilities and obligations.

And I let my mind wander. Now I was really free to think. My mind was not cluttered. I wanted to focus on getting better. I remembered what I'd been trying to do before I arrived. I'd been asking myself the same questions for seven years. I didn't think I was sick, but I also knew that what I had was obviously not like having a cold. What I wanted to do most was figure out this strange situation—*What did the voices of my family and friends want from me, and was I in any kind of trouble?*

Sitting on my new bed, I made peace with being at McLean. I didn't like being locked up, but I was fine, right? I still heard a few words here and there from the voices, but they were very faint. The voices were mostly gone since I'd arrived in a new place. The mind works in wondrous ways. I looked out the window at the trees, at the snow, and thought some more. It was the middle of the winter. *I am stuck here.*

A nurse came in and interrupted my thoughts. She gave me a piece of paper with more information about the hospital. She told me about the classes scheduled for the day. "Try to go to a few classes!" she said encouragingly as she walked out of my room. I didn't listen to her. I felt very tired. All I wanted was to sleep.

A girl walked in, my roommate, while I was lying in my bed, trying to nap. I opened my eyes when I heard her. We said hello. She smiled. She might have been in her teens. She was halfway through braiding her curly black hair into thin threads. "I think it's cool you can do that. I've done that once before with my straight hair. Very painful," I said.

She smiled. "Oh, it's easy," she said. I liked her instantly. We stayed together in the room without speaking anymore, and I fell asleep.

At some point, I got up from my nap. I realized I had no idea what time it was. I couldn't find any clock in my room, and I wasn't wearing a watch. I went out of the room and explored the rest of the unit, looking for a clock. I found the nurse station, the kitchen, and the dining room. I found an art room and a piano in one of the hallways. There was also a TV room. I found a clock at the nurse station and realized I'd missed lunch. Luckily, I wasn't hungry. When I was not on my medication, I ate much less.

There were maybe ten to fifteen other patients of various ages in this unit from what I could see. Everyone was free to walk about or stay in their rooms. In addition to patients, there were many nurses and mental health specialists walking about. We were all mixed together.

I wanted to take a shower. I got a towel, soap, and shampoo from the nurse station and took a shower in one of the common bathrooms. I had to figure out how to turn on the water. It was a bit awkward standing in a strange place, completely naked, trying to turn on the water. Once it was on, the water was not hot at all. It was going to be a cold shower. It didn't matter. Usually I showered every day, sometimes twice a day. It always relaxed me. I felt much better after the shower, even though it was a bit chilly.

After the shower, I went back to my room. The place felt so novel to me yet it was just like a dorm with shared rooms and bathrooms. At this point, I wasn't trying to figure out how I'd arrived at the hospital anymore. I was trying to focus on the problem, and I was trying to solve it. My life problem. The voices. My mind wandering again. Then someone interrupted me. A young male patient who couldn't have been older than college-aged came to me and said, "You have a phone call."

"What? Oh. Where?"

"The pay phone is on the other side, down the hall."

"Thanks." At the phone booth, I picked up the phone. "Hello?" I said quietly. Immediately, I heard Chris's excited voice coming through the line. He'd moved to Hong Kong about three or four years before. In the past, if there was anything wrong with me, everyone called Chris, and he would come and find me. I guessed someone had called him again. Now he was too far away to come in person.

"Hello! What did you do? Why are you so stupid and got yourself into a hospital?" he said. He sounded very upset.

"I was trying to figure things out." I didn't feel it was bad to get into a hospital.

"Why don't you just take your pills? I don't know what to say to you anymore."

"How do you know I'm in a hospital?"

"Levina called me."

"How are you? What are you doing?" I said, trying to have a normal conversation. I couldn't believe he was calling me from Hong Kong.

"You want to know what I'm doing? I'm reading!" He got loud again, and then he sighed.

"What are you reading?" I wanted this conversation to be like one on any other day.

Getting very excited again, he said, "I really don't know what to do with you. You want to know what I'm reading? I'm reading *The Girl with the Dragon Tattoo*. So, what are you going to do now?" He definitely did not want to talk about himself.

"I don't know," I said in a quiet voice. I'd read that book. I didn't know Chris read books like that. Why was he yelling? I hated being yelled at.

"Why don't you think about what you do before you do things? Or you wouldn't end up in a hospital! You are so stupid! You..."

I hung up the phone. I felt bad hanging up on him, but I didn't want to hear him yelling at me anymore. Maybe I didn't know what I was going to do yet, but I would figure it out for myself. I waited a few minutes, sitting alone in the phone booth. I stared at the phone. It didn't ring again. He didn't call back. I walked back to my room.

Time flew by fast. My first night at the hospital came. I was lying in bed with my eyes closed. The door to the room was opened, and the light from the hallway lit up a small part of the room. Someone tapped my shoulder. I opened my eyes to look at the person. A nurse stood next to my bed in the dark with three small plastic cups in her hand. She told me what they were. "This one is medication. This is a vitamin. This is water." Thus began my first conversation about my treatment plan in the hospital. It was a short one.

"I don't want to take it," I said to the nurse. I took the water. I swallowed the vitamin. I gave her back the empty water cup. And then I lay back down in bed and closed my eyes. I thought: *What if all the voices I heard were real? What if the medication was just a way to cover them up? What might chemicals do to a healthy brain? The medication could block my good synapses. Would that make my brain slow?* I wanted to make sense of what I thought, heard, saw, and felt. Maybe the doctors could help me prove something about the brain one way or another. I didn't want to waste my efforts. I wanted to continue to search for the truth.

The nurse went away without forcing me to take the medication. I was thankful. I'm still surprised by it, but it was the right choice. For too many years I had been told to take medication without understanding how it was affecting my brain. I still heard distant voices when I went to bed, but I was able to have a good first night's sleep at McLean.

The next morning, I got up around 7:30. This was early for me. Maybe it was because of the light through the windows, maybe it was the bed, maybe it was because I hadn't taken any medication. A young woman came to me right when I got up and asked, "Would you come with me?" I nodded even though I didn't know where she was taking me. I was brought to the end of the hall. There was an empty chair in front of a semicircle of seated people. Some of them had paper and pens. Some of them wore white uniforms. I was told that this was my treatment team. My treatment team included an attending psychiatrist, a resident psychiatrist, a medical student, a primary care nurse, a clinical case manager/social worker, and a mental health specialist. One of the professionals was Jerry, the stranger I'd run into in the hallway when I first arrived. He was my nurse. The young woman who had come to get me that morning was my medical student.

I sat down in the empty chair in front of my team. Everyone looked friendly. They introduced themselves. I heard their names but immediately forgot most of them. The resident psychiatrist started the conversation. "How are you feeling?"

"I'm good," I said. I gave a short description of what I was experiencing. My team asked me why I thought I was there, why I hadn't wanted to take medication the night before, and if I could focus or not. I said I was there because I had gone to the ER, and they sent me here. I said I didn't want to take medication if my brain was healthy. I didn't have trouble focusing or talking that morning with my treatment team. It felt like a normal chat and great to have a team of people interested in me. I talked to them for about fifteen minutes. After we were finished, I went back to my room. I started getting ready for a shower. Despite what Chris had said, I wasn't worried about being locked up in a hospital. I was starting a new morning routine: I got up, I talked to these people, I took a shower, and then I was free to do whatever I wanted.

At some point during the day, the medical student came to me again. She wanted to talk to me more. She took me to a private room and closed the door behind her. We both sat down next to a table. "How are you doing?"

"I'm fine. Thanks."

"Do you know why you are here?" she asked softly.

"I do. I was in the middle of trying to figure out what was happening around me. I was adjusting how I think and behave about different things." I wanted to tell her my problems. I wanted her to understand what I was thinking. I tried to explain.

"Do you take medication?"

"No, I'm not right now. That's what I was trying to figure out. If my brain is healthy, and I take medication, that would be bad for me. I want to make sure I definitely need it. I feel fine right now."

"Okay. Thank you." She stood up, and I followed, and we left the room together.

I had the whole day in front of me. But I could sit and think only for so long. There was a new class schedule on my desk. I looked through all the classes and decided I would try to go to the class in the afternoon called "Communication." It was not at all what I expected. There were five of us, including the instructor, sitting around a table in the middle of a small room. The instructor was a man much older than me. He looked a bit like Santa Claus. He talked slowly. He talked about speaking our minds and expressing opinions. He asked everyone in the room to share something with the group. After everyone shared, the class ended.

At around four or five in the afternoon on my first day, my mental health specialist came and asked me to follow her into a tiny room. "How was your day?" she asked. I noticed the room had a guitar. I wondered who played. I rocked slightly forward and backward in the rocking chair. The day had gone well. I was in a good mood. For a few hours, I forgot about my problems. I wasn't hearing any voices. I had everything I needed in a safe place, and I was fine.

The morning conversations happened every morning except during weekends. The treatment team always started the dialogue by asking how I was doing. The conversations never felt scary or aggressive. It was easy for me to let the team know how I was doing from one day to the next. Every day I made small changes, we talked about it, and they kept track of my progress. I liked my team. Each evening someone always checked in with me to close out the day. They had a rotating schedule. After living alone, I suddenly found myself surrounded by a community in the hospital.

While I felt the care from the doctors and nurses and the friendliness from the other patients, I still couldn't understand why none of my family and friends were coming to get me out. *Do they think this is good for me?* Even though I wasn't trying to escape, I didn't think I should be locked up. *Why is no one on my side?* I felt I was standing up for myself by myself.

Levina was my first visitor. She came on my second night at the hospital. I met her in college, but I'd been friends with her all my years in Boston. When I was with Levina, she usually brought out the strength, logic, and confidence in me. When she came to the hospital, she brought me a brown shopping bag full of books, soap, pens, and a notebook. She expected I would have a lot of free time. She knew I liked to read. I had wanted a notebook, so I could write down my thoughts and get organized. I was surprised she knew about this, but she had a way of getting to what I was thinking. She seemed happy to see me and asked how I was. I told her what had happened so far in the hospital. I didn't ask her why no one was trying to help me leave. I didn't want to be confrontational, but I wanted to start speaking my mind. So I tried to tell Levina as much as I could. When she was leaving, I thanked her for coming to visit me and bringing me things.

After she left, I stopped feeling like the happy friend I'd been while she'd been there. I thought about my secret world. Only when I was alone did that secret world appear so completely in my mind.

The next day Samantha came. "We're taking turns taking care of your cats so not to worry," she told me as soon as she saw me. I had the habit of leaving my spare keys with a few close friends just in case I locked myself out. Samantha had picked up both underwear and simple outfits for me. Again, I shared with her everything about the hospital. I told her I was fine. When my friends asked me, I was always fine, never not fine. Samantha had a way of bringing out the most confident part of me. With her, I still didn't express any of my frustrations. I didn't know how to express the anger that was slowly building up inside, but I wanted to. For me, it was easier to talk positively about what was happening without getting emotional, so

I didn't talk about Joe and his world, the voices of my friends and family, the signs and sounds and games. I still didn't know how to merge these two very separate worlds.

On the third day, Maggie came and brought me more clothes and a clock. Maggie didn't usually say much about herself, but like my other friends, she never stopped asking me how I was. In the hospital, I didn't wear a watch and was having a difficult time knowing what time it was. Maggie brought me a black table clock. I had no idea how she knew I needed one. She brought me new comfortable outfits she'd picked out from Target, a guidebook to Paris since she knew I liked traveling and we'd gone to Paris together a few years before, and a picture of Brady, her dog. She wanted to remind me of happy things in our lives. Similar to Samantha and Levina, Maggie also worked full-time and had to make the trip to see me after work. Again, I felt thankful a friend had come.

However, mixed with my gratitude was anger. I had a very hard time being mad at Maggie, but I wanted so much to be mad at her for what she'd done. After she left, I threw the guidebook of Paris in the garbage can. Everything she did came back to me. She called the EMTs on me. She called my parents, so now they were worried. I decided that even though she was a nice person, she thought I was stupid and incompetent. She had violated my independence and control over my own life. When she brought me flowers on Valentine's Day, I took all the flowers, walked out of my room, and started handing them out to different patients and nurses. Everyone was looking for a cup to put their flowers in.

Samantha, Vara, Zoe, and Paige visited me next. The conversation we had together resembled ones we had when we all went out for dinners. After a while, the topic shifted to me. "How are you?" one of my friends asked.

I felt a sense of anger rising in me. "I'm very upset about what's happening to me," I said. "I don't know why EMR kept showing up at my apartment. Three times. They came and knocked on my door three times. Why?" I was shaking. My heart raced faster. I was learning to speak up about my frustration. I was not good at it.

Zoe immediately asked, "How can we help?" I felt all my anger subside.

"I don't know…" Later on, I realized what I wanted—for them to ask me what to do instead of doing things for me without my input. "Be asked!" I shouted in my head.

On Sunday, Ahmed and his wife Paivi brought their baby when they visited me. The little baby played on the bed next to me as we chatted. I thought, *This place must not be a bad place if a baby can come and play.* Ahmed handed me a few magazines on meditation and mindfulness. By this time, I had been given eight books of all different kinds. Some I would have picked out myself, some less likely. The books reminded me of my friends. After they left, I looked at the magazines, failing to connect medication and mindfulness to my situation.

My parents visited on Sunday too. Dad called ahead and asked if I wanted him to bring anything. I was craving pizza, a change from all the nutritious food at the hospital. "Pizza! Can you bring me pizza?" When my dad and stepmother came, they brought pizza and a plant. They wanted to know how I liked the hospital, if I was comfortable, if I was missing anything. They told me they cleaned my apartment and changed the litter for the cats. "They're fine at home. Don't worry," they said.

I thought it was so strange my father was not upset for me, that no one was fighting the doctors and nurses for me. But, even though I felt I was fighting a battle of my own, I didn't feel alone or isolated. Almost every day people came, good friends or my parents. A nurse was amazed at the support I was getting and said, "You have so many people visiting you all the time!" I became thankful for my friends again. Later, I found out that when I was first admitted to the hospital, Samantha told everyone they should coordinate, rotate, and come see me.

While my care team, friends, and family looked after me, I sorted through my thoughts. I sat at the desk and wrote my first entry at the hospital in my new notebook.

Thursday, Feb 10, 2011

I can't help but feel that I am being helped in more ways than I realize.

People can live on very little. Survival requires only shelter, food, and some social support. From all the materials and possessions that we have, I wonder how many people are truly happy.

How do I resolve experiences from the past and move forward in the best way that I can? How do I understand where I am today?

I am at a psychiatric hospital in a restricted unit.

I thought of a backpack my dad had with everything he needed to survive on a one-month hike. Health was so much more important than all my material possessions. Without being healthy, there was pretty much nothing I could do.

The next day I wrote:

Friday, Feb 11, 2011

How can I get help based on what I think the problem is?

I don't think there is one person in this world who can understand everything that I am going through. If I go to a doctor, he will focus on biology. If I go to a detective, he will focus on evidence. Should I take all the little things and connect the dots myself? Should I break down the problem and solve it piece by piece? Should I let others help me while I have no way of validating their recommendations and the information they are basing their decisions and actions on?

I can't check on everyone. I can't even check on me.

I was trying to figure out why I was in the hospital. I was trying to remember what I did before coming to the hospital. But I could only remember bits and pieces. The past didn't flow into a neat sequential timeline. Among fuzziness, some details stood out. I remembered hearing the phrase "That confirms it!" It must have been a response to something I was thinking at the time. I also remembered a friend asking me to call her when I was alone in my bedroom. "Call me, Mindle! I have not heard from you in a long time. Call me!" The voice of my friend was urgent. I remembered how I behaved with people I'd met around the time when I had my first breakdown. It stood out in my mind how awkward I had been and how unusual. I remembered how I felt when I was taking the T home alone from a movie. I ran after being startled by the people at the movie.

There were more disjointed details. I desperately wanted to make sense out of them. I started making lists. I tried to organize my memories.

I thought about the pill I was taking before being in the hospital. The pill somehow stopped people signaling to me on the street, acting weird in restaurants, walking toward me. It stopped my friends and family talking to me out of thin air. But the pill hadn't stopped me from hearing distracting noises at home. Even after I moved, those sounds did not stop. Also, the pill didn't stop someone poking me out of nowhere.

I drifted in and out of my memories.

Without hearing my voice friends, it was easy to be normal, to forget my problems. I was able to do whatever I wanted. I found a treadmill at the hospital. I started jogging there. I was in good spirits. Other times I tried to figure out what was happening to me. I wrote down whatever was on my mind.

During my first weekend at McLean, I noticed there was a smaller team of caregivers in AB2 on the weekend, and it felt like a weekend even though I was not working. I decided to exercise. I felt inactive being inside AB2 for so many days. In my diary, I wrote: "Exercise makes me feel healthier. I have not been on a walk in five days. Walking on the treadmill for forty minutes got my heart rate up. I let it go for a while. Sweat. Circulation." I even borrowed a boombox from the nurse station to listen to music while I walked. Life felt normal and productive when I exercised.

Then I changed my mind about feeling normal at the hospital. On Sunday, I wrote: "It is amazing to see everyone here visiting. I want to be excited, like being at a house party. However, I am not. What goes on inside a place like this is doctors, nurses, and counselors doing checks. Vitals are taken. Plenty of food and snacks. All in the hope of making someone feel better, healthier. Open spaces. People getting to know each other with either words or silence." It was easy to notice that normal day-to-day things were hard to get in a locked facility. The young man who'd told me Chris called was listening to music in the hallway one day, and that made me miss my own playlist. I asked him to lend me his MP3 player, and he generously did. Another young man somehow ordered pizza delivery one night. I could smell it from all the way down the hall. I walked by, and he offered me a piece. I noted down my sentiment, "I realize that coke, pizza, and mp3 players are hard to come by."

Seeing my roommate with her fully braided hair brought me back to one of my trips in the Caribbean. I wrote: "Braiding hair is hard. Someone can always do something that I can't do. I'm glad I tried that in Tobago. A lot of work. Made my head look huge. It hurt. So not for me." Being in the hospital, I felt appreciative of the different types of people I met, trying different things and learning about different cultures.

Then my thoughts went to the future. I wrote: "I have been in the US for twenty-four years. And I think of myself as an American. But is it time for me to move to a new continent? Is my thinking beginning to be limited? To be normalized? I don't think so. I think my friends are diverse. And what the hell am I going to do with all this supposed diversity and open-mind-edness? Sitting here?" I wanted to give back to society. *I should do something useful and meaningful!*

I had spoken with Ahmed on the phone. I wrote, "Recap from conversation with Ahmed: (1) Life is stuck both personally and professionally. Not because I was not doing well. Have a ton of great friends and family. (2) My life experience has taken on quite a unique and abnormal path. Ugh. What is this? I definitely experienced and learned a bunch of weird stuff. Now what?!" At this time, even though life was stable, I felt I was standing still, doing the same things over and over again.

Then the next thought came back to me and my situation. "I am just one person. But there are many, many, many families, friends, and people out there. Well, if they are all up to some-thing, it would be a bit overwhelming." The power of people in numbers could be scary. Every one of my friends was trying to help me—they were each up to something. I felt overwhelmed by them.

As time went on, I was able to remember more about the past, the time right before I came to McLean, the time around my first breakdown, and in between. If what I thought was true, that people could talk to me out of thin air somehow, then there were many people who were part of my experience. *I know how I feel. I know what I hear and see. But am I right? Is it true?* Every time I remembered a new detail, I wrote it down, so I had a record of it. For instance, I took notes of games I'd played with the voices of my friends. I called this diary entry: "Games: Crazies Things from Last Week." In the first game, the voices of Ahmed, Paivi, and Jules were there. The game was "Pass It On." The way it worked was one person said either a phrase or a word to pass on to the next person. The next person continued the saying, and then another person took a turn. It was like a chain message. The voice of Ahmed said: "Everything I do." I said in response, "I do it for Daisy!" I had done this for hours while sitting in my apartment. Another game I'd played was "Name the Person." The trick was to listen to a song and see who the song reminded me of.

Mixed with remembering was being visited by my close friends. They did not leave me alone. On both Saturday and Sunday, Samantha, Zoe, Vara, and Paige visited me. I felt fortunate to have them visiting. I knew they had busy lives. I noted in my little notebook, "I admire my mom friends for working full-time, taking care of their families, and still having time to keep up with what's going on (with me)." I felt cared for.

While I was able to think freely and write, my friends continued to bring me a good dose of reality and incredible support. In this mental white space, I compared my life to theirs. I was still single and on a different life path. I thought about meeting new people and dating men. I wondered if I would ever have a family of my own, a husband and kids. *What will my future be?*

On Monday, February 14, 2011, the sixth day, I told my doctor I wasn't at the hospital voluntarily. I said I thought the reason for someone being committed to a hospital was if she was hurting herself or someone else. I was doing neither of those things. I didn't think I was seriously ill. I was told the name of the doctor who had admitted me. I said I didn't know that person. I didn't have any understanding of the law, but my instinct told me to make sure I was clear about my opinion on being locked up even though I was comfortable at the moment. I wanted to make sure I was heard.

Soon after, a nurse came by and gave me a piece of paper, which was a notice of my rights. I'd been admitted to the hospital because someone thought I needed to be there. The hospital could keep me for up to three days. At the end of this three-day period, the hospital had to either allow me to leave or ask a court to commit me for up to an additional six months, if the doctors at AB2 thought it was needed. The hearing would be within five business days after the three-day period. She also told me a lawyer representing me would be speaking to me soon.

A man of my height walked toward me while I was trying to get lunch and introduced himself. He said he was my attorney, and he would be representing me if I ended up going to a court hearing. He asked me to follow him to a meeting room, so we could discuss my situation in more detail. I was okay skipping lunch. The conversation I was going to have with him was much more important than food. We sat down, and he started to explain the rules to me.

"I read your records," he said. "If you go in front of a judge, it's basically your words against the doctors, your friends, and family. Before you came here, you wanted to quit your job. No matter what your reason was, the judge is going to see that you wanted to go from being independent to not. It's hard to argue against all that, and with everyone else. You don't have a high chance of winning."

*Will everyone in the hospital, my friends, and family all speak up against me in court?* I remembered telling Samantha and Ahmed I wanted to quit my job right before I'd been admitted to McLean. I had wanted to slow down, take a break, and recharge. Samantha immediately told me she thought it was a bad idea. Would they now use those random thoughts against me?

"The court hearing date is Thursday. It will be held downstairs."

"I don't want to go to court if I don't have to."

"Here is my card. Let me know what you decide. And feel free to call me if you want to discuss anything else."

In my head, while talking to the lawyer, I pictured myself being locked up for six months. I was worried about losing my apartment. If that happened, I'd end up on the street after I left the hospital. *Who will pay my bills? Take care of my things?* This could not get out of control. It just could not. This was not about how I got into the hospital anymore. This was about people thinking I needed help, and I had to follow the rules and be cooperative, so I could be released and get out of here. After I talked to the lawyer, I told the nurse I was staying. I didn't want to go to court and make this situation more complicated than was necessary. The doctors and I could work out what was best for me.

Soon after I told the nurse I was staying, I was given a piece of paper to sign. And that made it official. I was admitted to McLean voluntarily. I was there now to cooperate with everyone.

After talking to the lawyer the hospital provided for me, my friend Levina came to visit for the second time. As a lawyer, she proactively had done some research on the law for me. She asked if I knew the rules, probably guessing I was not prepared at all and didn't know my legal rights. She didn't know a lawyer had already talked to me that day. From my earlier conversation, I felt I had no choice in the matter, and I was already upset about what I'd learned about the law and about my compromise. When Levina wanted to talk about it more, I couldn't believe it and became furious.

"I did some research. The hospital can keep you here for three days. Then you have to sign in. And if you don't, then you have to go to court," she told me.

I kept silent.

"You can see the different forms." Levina handed me the legal forms she'd found online. I still didn't say a word. I took the forms but didn't look at them.

"Do you want me to help you get a lawyer to represent you? You will need a lawyer."

"I don't want a lawyer. I don't want to be locked up. But I guess I have to stay now," I finally said. There was tense silence.

Levian said, "Okay."

After Levina was gone, I immediately felt I had been unreasonable. She'd taken the time to check on me. She was on top of things. Later, when we had dinner, I apologized.

Once I signed the paper to stay at the hospital, the doctors focused on medication next. During our morning session, we talked about how I'd been feeling the day before, and I repeated the fact that I didn't take or want to take any medication. After the morning session ended, as everyone was leaving, the doctor tapped me on the shoulder to stop me from walking away. He was clean cut and probably middle-aged. As we both stood in the hallway facing each other, he said in a gentle and calm voice: "Have you considered the benefit of taking the medication? Consider the benefits." He gave me a smile, "Think about it." Then he went on to meet other patients.

Right before coming to the hospital, I thought I had almost proved the voices were real. If they were real, then I didn't need to take anything. I just needed to figure out how to shut them off. I was on a mission to discover my own remedy. But I was not so sure I could now.

As I was trying to figure out what I should think about next, my doctor made sure I was thinking about medication next. For a whole day, I thought about what the doctor had said after the morning session. I thought, *Consider the benefits.*

I felt very weighed down by the decision whether or not to take medication. It seemed that by taking medication, I would undo everything I had tried to accomplish in the last three months: all that work trying to find the truth within myself. To me, these tiny pills defined the difference between me as a sick person and me as a healthy person. If I didn't have to take the pill, then, in a way, I was undoing my first mental breakdown. I, not the pill, would have corrected whatever mistake I had made. Everything had started with the initial breakdown. I should have been mentally stronger when meeting Dan. I should have been smarter when I started thinking grandiose thoughts about music, books, and movies. I should have asked for help when I felt uncomfortable. I shouldn't have been so scared.

*Consider the benefits.*

In 2002, when it was first decided I would take medication, I wasn't an active participant in the discussion. Dr. Han had made the decision unilaterally. But I'd never thought medication was good. Chris always thought I had some weird phobia about taking it. Instinctively, I believed the less medication I took the better.

*Consider the benefits.*

The doctor had a good point. I needed to consider the benefits. Medication had benefits! What could I lose by trying again? Being at the hospital was the best place to experiment. I could track how I was doing before and after I took it. I could always tell the team I wanted to stop again. The hospital was a safe environment. Better here than doing this on my own at home.

*Consider the benefits.*

In my mind, something clicked. The medication could help with the voices. I started to internalize the meaning of being a schizophrenic. The voices were from my brain. *From me!* In my mind, I started replaying everything I'd heard on my own. I was speechless. I was trying to make sense of it all again but now in a different way. I realized there was actually nothing to learn from all of my memories. Because the happenings had all been just hallucinations. There were no interesting stories behind the memories. My brain had made up the voices and games. So, there was nothing to understand, nothing to be solved, and no meaning in any of it. I had a mental illness: a brain disease.

I thought, *Had it all really been meaningless?* My first therapist Susan had told me once, "If you think it's real, then it's real." I could not just discount what I experienced. My experiences and memories were important to me. They made me who I was. I needed more time to think through this.

But that afternoon I told the doctor I would like to take the medication. My decision was received with calmness. He explained there were three different medications I could take for what I had: Zyprexa, Risperdal, and Abilify. He compared their level of sedations and described their side effects. He also asked me about my past experiences. I explained about my weight gain while taking Zyprexa and also that I'd taken Abilify but how, for whatever reason, it hadn't worked out. The doctor mentioned I'd lost too much weight too quickly right before I came to the hospital. As long as I was hearing voices, I stopped paying attention to food. I learned that losing weight quickly could have harmed my kidneys. I could have damaged my body while focusing on proving whether or not the voices were real. I preferred not to have the artificial craving for food. The doctor decided to put me on Risperdal.

That night when the nurse came to give me my pill, I willingly took the medication.

The next morning I woke up feeling a bit groggy but not too bad. My head felt slightly heavier, as if I were wearing a heavy hat. The lightness in my head went away, and I felt dizzy getting out of bed. I made notes in my notebook about how differently I felt that morning.

On Wednesday, February 16, 2011, exactly one week after waking up the first time at AB2, I finally took the medication everyone had wanted me to take. I noticed the following: "It was harder to get up and go to the bathroom at 6:30 am; when I woke up my head felt heavy and sedated, and I had to work hard to wake up; regaining consciousness felt very abrupt and forceful when I needed to go to the bathroom; I felt more sensitive to noise while half-awake in bed; it was harder to think while in bed; my weight as of yesterday was 118 lb." I took notes because I wanted to make sure I knew exactly how the medication was affecting my body, knowing in a few days I would not be able to notice any difference.

On Tuesday, February 15, 2011, I watched TV for the first time in years. There was a live broadcast of Obama speaking about the budget at a daily press conference. I wrote, "He reads ten letters a day to stay in touch with people. He can't try to make everyone in America happy; as much as he would want to be a case manager, pick up the phone, and work with individuals, he can't. He has a tough job. How do you make two billion people happy!" Comparing his job with my life, suddenly my life seemed so manageable. He said, "We want to be on the right side of history. But we can't predict history." I never thought of using the word "history" as the "future." I definitely wanted to be on the right side of my future, if not my history.

Even though I had just gained such an important awareness about what my brain was capable of creating, I still wanted to understand and capture what it had done and what I'd experienced. I continued to reflect on the past. It was not easy to let go of it all just like that. For instance, I remembered rules I'd made up for myself during one of my psychotic episodes. I would cycle through these terms in my head with voices of different friends. *One time* (try everything at least once!), *try again* (don't give up too easily! Try everything at least two or three times), *keep trying* (don't give up too easily and do the same thing over and over and over again), *day one* (it's easy to start things! Keeping up the work is the hard part), and *two-second* (sometimes it's good to have a little patience). I'd felt inspired by these commands, shouting them in my head again and again. I recorded them in my diary. Even though I was questioning the meaning behind these memories, they still felt—and feel—precious.

The next morning the medical student came to get me for our morning session just like on the other days. I found my usual seat in front of the semicircle of people.

"You took the medication last night. How are you feeling?" the resident psychiatrist asked.

"Fine. The voices are gone. My brain feels a little heavier.

It was harder to get up this morning and during the night as well. I felt dizzy when I got up. But other than that, I feel fine." I explained the differences I was experiencing to my treatment team as clearly as I could.

"Those are all normal side effects. Since you are reacting well, I want to increase the dosage tonight. Okay?" the doctor said in a friendly way. He explained to me I'd be on a higher dosage of medication, which was what I needed to transition from the hospital to being on my own.

"Yes. Sounds good," I said and smiled back. During my future visits with future doctors, I would help them find me the right dosage and stabilize my medication like this. *Consider the benefits*, I would say to myself over and over again. I just hadn't wanted to end up being a drugged-up vegetable. The drugs could do that, but I trusted these doctors. I believed no one at the hospital would pretend I was sick if I wasn't. I had abandoned my attempts to prove that the voices were real.

As I talked with my treatment team, I realized again that taking medication traded one set of problems with another set of problems: side-effects. Then again, I said to myself: *Consider the benefits*.

Today I feel very grateful I was treated by my team. However, talking to other patients who were sent to other hospitals, I learned that my sole hospitalization experience was not the norm. I was lucky to be in Boston, to be sent to McLean.

On the seventh day I was in AB2, I saw people putting on their jackets and writing their names on the whiteboard in front of the nurse station. They were going out for walks. I ran back to my room and put on my jacket and shoes. I stood in front of the nurse station with everyone else and waited with them. The group was waiting for the walk group leader to show up, do a headcount, and take the group out.

"You can't go out," a nurse told me.

"Oh. How do I get to go out?" I asked.

"You will have to ask your nurse."

"Okay." I went back to my room and took off my jacket and shoes. *Oh well.*

I learned later that taking walks outside was a level two privilege, which also included being able to go to the gym and fitness center. I tried to go out one more time with the walking group, but the walking group leader always knew I wasn't allowed to go out yet.

"Can I go out for walks?" I asked my nurse when she came to visit.

"I'll have to speak to the treatment team about that. We'll see," she said.

"Okay." I guessed the only thing I could do was to ask. At least now she knew that I wanted to go out.

The next day my nurse said to me, "You can go out with the group now. You got level two." I didn't know how I had been promoted. But I was happy to be able to go outside.

I looked at the schedule for that day and noted the time for the walk. At the exact time, I was there with my jacket and shoes all ready to go. I'd been inside for seven days straight. A few more people joined me and gathered in front of the nurse station.

It was a warm spring day. I was dressed in my winter coat, but I didn't care. The fresh air hit my face. The sunlight shone so brightly. The sky was so blue. I tried to take it all in. I started chatting with the walk group leader. "It's nice out," I said.

"Yes, it's a beautiful day."

"It's the first time I am seeing the McLean campus."

"McLean Hospital started as a hospital with a farm. There are both inpatient and outpatient facilities here. I've been working here for a long time, many years." I saw signs of facilities for kids and elderly as well.

Many of the patients already had been on walks. They knew where to go and which way to turn. I didn't know where I was going and just followed the group around. I didn't like that feeling, following people around.

The second walk was much more enjoyable. I knew what to expect this time. During the walk, I saw the backs of young kids walking in front of me. I couldn't help but feel worried for them. They were so young and had so much more to learn about life, yet they already had challenges related to brain disease. I was glad my mental illness started when I was in my thirties. I felt I had a foundation of good life experience before I became sick. My positive life experience overall, prior to my first breakdown, made me who I was and helped me handle the challenges of my broken brain.

While walking, I saw two deer just standing among the trees on the hospital campus. I thought, *If the deer can live here, then this is a wonderful place.*

Besides walking, I continued to use the treadmill in the small room next to the nurse station. I wanted to exercise. I had plenty of time. So every day I would walk and jog on the treadmill for thirty to forty-five minutes. I even found a radio I could borrow from the nurse station, so I had music while I jogged.

A young boy, maybe in his teens, saw me jogging. He got excited about it too. He started following me around. A couple of times, he waited for me to finish then jumped on the treadmill himself. He was a big guy with very big feet. When he was on the treadmill, he made loud thumping sounds. The mental health specialist was not as comfortable with him walking and jogging on his own. "Be careful. Don't hurt your right foot. You know you have to be careful with it." The boy had been in and out of the hospital a few times by this time.

One day, during dinner, another boy excitedly shared that he had just finished writing a song. It was rap. Someone urged him to show it to us, so he started to rap in the cafeteria. Everyone, including the hospital staff, enjoyed it.

A college girl came to the hospital a bit after me. She'd discovered she was not well and drove herself to McLean. After an intake downstairs, she was admitted. We started talking about books because she saw me reading. "I like reading too, especially a good story. But I don't like reading textbooks." I lent her a romantic novel that Maggie had brought me. The college girl was sure she would enjoy it.

My roommate got discharged. She was a teenager with a second kid coming. I hadn't even known why she was at the hospital. I never asked, and she'd never said. "Good luck with everything," I said.

"Yeah. Thanks. It will be good to see my daughter. Want to see a picture of her?" I looked through the photo album, which was obviously very precious to her. She seemed like a happy person who did not have a lot.

"Is someone coming to pick you up?" I asked, handing back her photo album.

"Yeah. My mom should be coming."

"Congrats on leaving here."

"Yeah. I'll have to figure out some stuff. See what I am going to do with a second kid." I gave her a hug as she packed up everything she had into two paper bags.

A woman walked into our room. She didn't have any bags with her. "Hi, I guess I'm your new roommate. My name is Kim. Hi Mindy." Kim was talkative and lively. She told me about her history right away. She got mixed up with drugs, which ended the career she'd had as a real estate agent. "But I'm feeling better now. I'm doing better," she said and told me about her medication.

"I'm glad you're doing well," I told her.

There was a constant flow in and out of patients. The unit had no trouble managing everyone in a very orderly fashion. Every day I would see who was new and who was gone. There were people of all ages. And everyone had a story. I learned more about life from almost everyone I met.

I remember one afternoon I was sitting in front of the nurse station, reading an article from the *New Yorker*. A man had devoted his life to looking at snowflakes. *All snowflakes start the same*, he wrote. It was their travels that made them change and become different. They became what they became until they melted. Every one of them would melt. I thought, *People are just like snowflakes*. I thought how much I liked meeting people and learning about their "travels." But meeting people in the hospital was different. In the hospital, it was not about what kind of coffee you liked to drink but what medication you took.

By the time I'd been in the hospital for a week, I felt so clear in my head that I started to think about how I could leave. I'd seen a few people get discharged already. Some people were there for just a long weekend; some had been there for more than one month. I didn't know how long I needed to stay. I felt fine. I was taking medication. I didn't know if there was anything else I needed to work out with the doctors. I was ready to get out and resume a normal life.

"When can I leave here?" I asked my nurse.

"You need to ask your case manager. She's in charge of your discharge plan," he said.

"Oh. Okay."

At the next morning session with my treatment team, we started with the usual question. "How are you?" the medical student asked.

"Good," I said.

"What did you do yesterday?"

"I went to a music class. I read. I watched some talk shows on TV."

"Were you able to follow the talk show?"

"The talk show these days? No. Not at all!"

Everyone burst out laughing.

I thought of my question. When the morning chat wrapped up, I asked the treatment team, "When can I leave?" I smiled a big smile. No one looked surprised at my question. They all smiled back.

"I'm working on your discharge plan. I will share with you what I have when it's ready," my case manager answered.

She came to me that afternoon and told me about the plan she'd put together for me. "You will start the partial day program at McLean after you're discharged. The day program runs from 9 am to 3 pm. We will discharge you on Thursday of this week. You'll have to check in with them Friday morning. I've also made an appointment for you for an intake with the Freedom Trail Clinic. They're in downtown Boston. Here's the date and time of your first appointment and whom you will meet with. Here's all the information you'll need. Let me know if you have any questions. Okay?" She handed me a folder and smiled.

"Okay. Sounds good." I was actually thinking, *Why am I not done yet?* But I was willing to learn. I'd made a request to her earlier that I wanted to see a doctor in the city even though it would have been wonderful to see the same doctors I knew at McLean. Downtown would be more convenient for me. She told me in the downtown clinic the caseworkers partnered closely with the psychiatrist. I liked that idea. I wouldn't have to worry about passing messages between the two professionals. I remembered trying to connect everyone from different roles before I'd come to the hospital.

During my last two days in the hospital, I started giving my stuff away to other people who needed or wanted them. I had everything I needed at home. I passed on the alarm clock, skin products, magazines, and some books. I also took down contact information from the other patients. I didn't know if our paths would cross again, but it felt good to write down a few emails and phone numbers.

On Thursday, February 24, 2011, after being in the hospital for two weeks and one day, I packed my clothes, a plant from my parents, my notebook, hospital papers, and books into two brown paper bags. I had planned to take the bus home, but none of my friends would let me leave on my own, so I had to wait for my cousin to come in order to leave. I hugged my roommates and hospital-mates and said goodbye. I waved to the nurses and said thank you. A few people congratulated me. I waited next to the door in front of the nurse station with my brown paper bags. I guessed I would have looked a little ridiculous on the bus with my bags.

My cousin Chao came around 1 pm. We hugged each other. He picked up my bags. I wasn't sad even though I would miss the hospital. I would miss all the familiar faces and community. I marched through the door on my way back to my normal life. I remember feeling that I was closing a part of my life and starting something new.

I was happy to see Chao. I shared with him how cared for I felt. I talked about what I should do next according to my treatment team. The car ride home was quick. The music was on. I talked most of the way, sharing with him my current state of mind. He dropped me off at home. I assured him I was going to be okay on my own.

I opened the door to my apartment. I put down my bags and went into the kitchen. I sat down at one of the chairs. I looked out my window. I was alone for the first time in two weeks. If I counted the voices of my friends and family, it would be the first time I'd been alone in three and a half months. It was good to be home. I noticed a few things had been moved. My parents and friends had been at my place. I hoped they'd been comfortable here. My mail was piled up on the table. I hoped there was nothing urgent. The litter for the cats seemed to be the wrong kind. Regardless, my cats seemed to be happy to see me.

I didn't have any plans for the next day. I hadn't thought that far ahead.

I was alone. And it was very quiet. The quietness felt shapely and distinct.

I thought, *What is the first thing I want to do? I want ice cream!* I took my wallet, phone, and keys with me and walked out of my apartment. It felt so good to be able to do that, to go where I wanted to go. I went to a Ben and Jerry's nearby in the mall. I bought one scoop of strawberry ice cream. It was wonderful.

That night Samantha came over for dinner. "How are you feeling?"

"Good. I feel good. It was good to have gone to the hospital. I feel like now I'm in a better position to deal with what I have. I still have a lot to think about."

"Yeah? Like what?"

"I feel like I'm unstuck from the past. I also got help. Proper help. I have a good idea what I need if I have an emergency. I have the proper support. I feel good."

"That's great. I'm glad you feel better."

After she left, I was alone. I noticed how quiet it was in the apartment. My phone rang. It was Maggie.

My phone rang again. It was Vara.

My phone rang again. It was my dad.

I was now home, out of the hospital, with freedom, thinking about all the people who had been with me in the hospital during the last two weeks. Somehow, my friends and family all knew I was home. I repeated over and over again how good I felt to everyone who called. Everyone was happy for me and promised to meet up soon.

It was very quiet again after the phone calls. It was such a strong contrast to not having several voices talking to me nonstop and to not having ten to twenty people constantly around me like at the hospital. I thought, *How quickly I'd gotten used to them in such a short time. Now I need to get back to living my normal life.* I felt lucky and grateful. I was fortunate to have been at McLean. Of course, I hadn't planned any of these events, yet I had been through them. I felt peaceful sitting in my kitchen. I felt thankful to be home. I was blessed to regain my freedom.

## MEDICAL RECORD: DISCHARGE SUMMARY 02/24/2011

My care team was also optimistic about my discharge. Here is what was documented:

> The patient was admitted on Wednesday, 02/09/11, to the inpatient Bipolar and Psychotic Disorders Unit at McLean Hospital under a Section 12 status.

> By discharge, the patient was agreeable to continue

risperidone pharmacotherapy and expressed an understanding that she would need to closely follow up with
a therapist and psychiatric prescriber as an outpatient.
Significant discussion was spent with the inpatient team
inquiring as to when the patient might be able to stop
the medication, and the patient agreed that she would
take this medication for a significant amount of time,
many months, after discharge and would only go down
on the medication under the advice of a psychiatric prescriber. The patient was looking forward to discharge on
discharge day and described preparing for her life after
the hospital by arranging to scale back on her work load
upon return to work and staying with a friend during
the days immediately following her discharge.

Condition on discharge: Improved. Discharge examination was significant for pleasant and cooperative
behavior. The patient was neat, clean, and well groomed
in appearance with good eye contact. Her mood was
"excited," and her affect was full and pleasant with a
slight presentation of anxiety. Her thought processes
were linear and easy to follow, and her thoughts focused
on the fact that, "I'm excited to go as I have a lot to do
outside the hospital." The patient denied suicidality or
homicidality and denied thinking that anyone was out
to get her. The patient denied auditory hallucinations.
The patient was grossly oriented and demonstrated fair
insight into her condition with fair judgment.

Aftercare treatment plans: The patient has an intake
with the McLean Behavioral Health Partial Hospital
Program at 8 am on 02/25/11. The patient was further

referred to the Freedom Trail Clinic for an intake at 1 pm on 03/14/11.

## MCLEAN DAY PROGRAM

After checking out from the hospital, I was enrolled in the partial day program at McLean for the next two weeks starting the very next day. I was told this would help me make the transition back to a normal routine. I was told it was better to have structure in my days. I think this was helpful for people who normally could not put together a routine themselves. I had a job waiting for me to get back to. I wasn't worried about structuring my days, but I didn't say anything. I thought I should follow the process and recommendations from my case manager and see how the program might help me.

On Friday, I took the bus to McLean and checked in with my greeter. I met with my new case manager, who was also responsible for running the whole program. He went through my schedule with me, which had been personalized. On a sheet of paper, he checked off classes of topics he thought were most relevant while explaining what they were. Then he handed me my class schedule for the week. The classes started at 9 am and ended at 3 pm. In addition to meeting in groups, I also had one-on-ones with my new psychiatrist and mental health specialist during the week. It felt like I was back in high school.

There were many other people there, similar to me, getting education on mental health. Many of them had also just finished staying at a secured unit. I found out there was another unit exactly like mine upstairs from where I'd stayed. Most people in my classes were from that unit. Again, I felt the busyness of McLean here, which felt similar to being at AB2, of having people constantly coming and going. Being there, I soon realized how little I knew about mental health and how much more I needed to learn. I took plenty of notes.

The classrooms were of different sizes with chairs arranged in circles along the walls. The instructor usually talked in the front of the room, sometimes giving out handouts, sometimes using the whiteboard. Some instructors were funny, some serious or friendly. They took attendance, so they could keep track of who showed up for classes. Other than that, it was an honor system. I was responsible and expected to be where I needed to be.

Hearing other people share their experiences made me realize how fortunate I was. A young woman in her early twenties had tried to kill herself because she was so depressed. She had struggled with living since she was a young teen. A man in his forties hadn't been able to make it out of his house for the past five years. He was trying to get a job now. He would have to find a way to explain the gap on his resume. Everyone had a story to tell and different challenges they were learning to manage.

Many people had been to a hospital more than once. Someone said: "When someone has cancer, everyone brings a cake. When someone gets checked into a mental hospital, no one comes. No one wants to talk about the problem." Luckily for me, this had not been the case.

I also felt very lucky about reacting well to my medication, even with some side-effects. A girl shared her experience of trying many different medications, hoping that something would help her. It was hard for the doctors to give her a diagnosis, to pinpoint what was wrong. I learned that sometimes no medications worked. People just had to manage their symptoms. I thought about how different my life would be if I had to live with my voices.

The goal was to keep out of the hospital—that was what

I learned from the other patients. I didn't want to enter their cycle of going in and out of hospitals like through a revolving door. I also didn't want to end up in assisted homes. If I didn't take care of myself, it could happen to me.

I learned a new way to look at what I did every day. I came up with four categories of activities I should aim to include: social, mastery, self-care, and pleasure. Social activities included interactions with people, such as going to the movies, meeting up at cafés, and having dinner together. Mastery activities were tasks I must do, such as laundry. Self-care included exercising, taking medications, having a good diet, and getting a good night's sleep. Pleasurable activities concerned doing fun things. An activity could cover more than one category. For example, I could enjoy exercising, which could count as both self-care and pleasure. Or, for me, going out to dinner with girlfriends was both social and pleasurable. The key thing to remember was to spend some time doing each category every day in order to be a balanced person. Activities mapped to categories differently for everyone. What I considered to be fun might not be fun to another person.

I also learned that unstructured time led to negative thoughts, bad behaviors, and then anxious emotions, and these thoughts, behaviors, and emotions led to more unstructured time. It became a vicious cycle. One technique I learned at McLean to avoid this was to organize my time or schedule. Since I was a project manager, scheduling was very easy and natural to me. I already did this in my life. Since my college days, every year I bought a calendar that kept all my appointments. I wouldn't have known what to do if I hadn't had my calendar. I was a big fan of this technique.

Typically, I thought I needed motivation before I did something: *motivation precedes action*. However, at McLean, I learned this could be flipped around: *let action precede motivation.* Instead of waiting to feel like going to the gym, schedule a gym time and just go. Once I started working out, I would feel good about it.

Cognitive therapy was different from behavior therapy. It told me I should accept negative emotions because they were part of life. Instead of focusing on how emotions affect behavior, I could use the following safety checks: *Will doing this raise my health insurance rates? If yes, don't do it!* Also: *Can I do what I want in public and conquer the feeling of embarrassment or awkwardness?* This was referred to as social experiment or exposure therapy. For example: *Buy a cup of coffee at Starbucks with all of my coins even when I know everyone behind me is waiting and might get annoyed. Other people don't like it. So what!* This matched my experience. Looking back to my first breakdown, I believed a big trigger had been that I wasn't comfortable with my own thoughts and feelings. Because I liked Dan, I had emotional conflicts within myself every time I ran into him. My thoughts made me anxious and unwell. I had to become comfortable with having emotions that were uncomfortable. *I liked him. So what!*

Mood monitoring focused on how I thought, felt, and acted in a specific situation. I learned that emotions fed into behaviors, which fed into thinking, which fed back to emotions. They were all connected. Affecting one would affect the other two. Mood monitoring was an exercise I could do to understand my own automatic thinking and how that automatic thinking translated into my behaviors and emotions. With that understanding, I could then change the way I thought. This also matched with things I'd been trying to figure out. For instance, I thought a young man had blocked me from going to the bathroom at a supermarket. Most likely, he was just in a hurry and needed to use the bathroom. From that thought about the one young man, my mind connected dots and imagined a group of boys had been playing tricks on me. Even though I didn't believe it and wanted to prove it was wrong, my automatic thinking was still mistaken. I had to undo what I thought.

Lastly, I learned about relapse management. The first phase was the pre-contemplation and denial phase. "Everything is fine" during this phase. Second was the recognition of a problem or contemplation. Third was the decision to make a change. The fourth phase was taking action and doing something about the condition. Then came the hard part: keeping it up, the maintenance, until symptoms recurred and possibly brought back denial. The cycle repeated.

For the first time I learned about the importance of staying well and not triggering another episode. In the seven years prior to my hospitalization, I knew there was a problem, and I wanted to do something about it, but I was not taking the right actions. I didn't know that with each episode, my brain would deteriorate a bit more. I didn't know that by looking for Joe and his world, I might break my brain even more. My last episode finally gave me the chance to think through my experience. With fresh memories of what I'd been through, the hospital stay gave me time and forced me into stages two and three. Now, I was taking the proper action! And the goal was to stay in maintenance mode for as long as possible.

After two weeks living in the hospital and two more weeks of attending the day program at McLean, I started living completely on my own again. However, I was on a mission now with my new understanding and realization. I wanted to learn everything I could about schizophrenia.

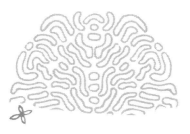

— Part 3 —

# ME, LATER

# 8

# LEARNING AND SHARING

## VOICE-FREE AGAIN

After completing the care and treatment at McLean, I went through a very different transition and outpatient routine than what I had with Dr. Han after my first breakdown. To start, I had a routine. My first and only breakdown had felt so much more severe. Now I was receiving so much more care and attention. It felt like such a luxury.

My chief psychiatrist at the day program wrote a letter to Medullan recommending I go back to work on a part-time basis. I had never worked less than full-time. I was hesitant about this recommendation, but my psychiatrist was insistent. "You should slowly transition back to the community," he said as he was getting ready to discharge me from the day program. *Transition back to the community?* His words threw me off as I said them a few more times in my head. It was unfamiliar to me to be treated this way. I was ready to go back to work, but I kept an open mind. The doctor knew best.

I made a lunch date with Ahmed, my good friend and CEO of Medullan, near where I lived. We sat at a free bench together while I gave him the letter and told him what the doctor had said. Ahmed did not hesitate at all in fully supporting me and my discharge plan. Even though it would be scaled down, I would still have an income. So after the day program finished at McLean, I was able to go right back to work part-time, twenty hours a week.

I was also fortunate I'd had a job before I went to McLean. My insurance through work with Blue Cross Blue Shield covered all of my healthcare costs, which were more than sixty thousand dollars. While I was at the day program, I started getting calls from a case manager at Blue Cross who wanted to know how I was doing and what my next step was. It was in both their interest and mine for me to get well and live independently again as soon as possible.

One day, on my way to work, I stood at the number 1 bus stop like I'd done for the past three years. All of a sudden I remembered, not heard, what my first voice Joe had said to me at that same spot maybe two years before. He'd said, "You should have gotten a jacket." At the time I felt thankful someone was caring for me. Now I knew there was no one out there. It was strange to understand how my broken brain had been talking to me.

My social worker at McLean had set up an appointment for outpatient care as part of my discharge plan. On the scheduled date, I made my way to the Freedom Trail Clinic, which is a center that specializes in schizophrenia. I met Dr. Oliver Freudenreich, my new psychiatrist, and Deborah, my new therapist. They asked me many questions. They wanted to know what I had experienced and how I was doing. From that day on, I saw Dr. F and Deborah every six weeks or so. They had quickly become part of my life.

I now had a network of people caring for me. Deborah could easily stay in touch with Dr. F since they were both at the same clinic. I had also formed a good relationship with my primary care doctor, who was also in touch with Dr. F and Deborah. Prior to my hospitalization, I jumped from therapist to therapist, unable to connect with them on an emotional level and talk about the real problems I was facing. I had a psychiatrist who saw me once a year for ten minutes. That had all changed. Now I felt connected and grounded with my care team.

Dr. F was a tall man who always had a smile. He always said hi to me in the hallway when I waited to see him for our appointments. He made me feel comfortable and welcome, which allowed me to open up to him completely. He had a very good understanding of what people like me thought. In one of our early appointments, he looked straight at me and asked, "Are you thinking about cutting your pill in half and taking half the dose?" I had done that before but not anymore. It was good to know I had a doctor who could predict my actions. He understood me and why I behaved the way I behaved.

The big difference between Dr. Han and Dr. Freudenreich was that I could tell Dr. F about my worries, and I felt that he cared. He would have discussions with me. For instance, I told him I was concerned about gaining weight because of Zyprexa. He offered me two options. I could eat better and exercise more, or I could take another medication that might trim my appetite. I tried a second medication for a few weeks and didn't see any dramatic weight loss. I decided I didn't want to take a second medication and stopped. Dr. F was there for me while I tried and okay when I stopped. He gave me knowledge and choices.

Dr F also asked me to take blood tests regularly, which surprised me. I had never done that before with Dr. Han. I learned that Zyprexa had side-effects that required monitoring. Dr. F needed to see how my body was reacting to my medication over time. For some patients on certain medications, they had to do blood work every two weeks. Luckily, my checkups were needed less frequently. I felt that Dr. F had a more comprehensive care plan in taking care of people like me. So, on some days, I fasted and went in for blood tests at the clinic.

One time, when work was busier than usual, I asked him if I could just call him for our appointment. When we met, we usually just had a conversation. We could do that with a phone call. He said, "Absolutely not. I need to see you. It's important that I see you in person." I realized how well I looked mattered to Dr. F. I also had asked him if I could see him less frequently. He said, "No. I need to see how you are doing with medication. Sometimes a lot can change in a few weeks." I couldn't help but think how different his approach was compared to the approach of Dr. Han, who saw me once a year and only asked me how my mother was doing!

With Deborah, I learned to talk about myself. Our time together was for me. She wanted to know what was on my mind. I was surprised she didn't want to talk about schizophrenia. She wanted to get to know me. At the beginning, I told her about my family and friends. Then I told her I was having trouble with working part-time. I wanted to make a plan, to be productive, to achieve something more. She made a comment: "You need to be comfortable with yourself. Enjoy your free time. It's for you. You don't have to be productive all the time. Slow down!" After speaking to her, I learned to give myself permission to slow down, not to work all day, to think about what I wanted to do besides working. Then I talked more about my friends, work, vacations, and starting to date again. By now, she knew about my parents and close friends. She had a sense of what I liked and didn't like. I never prepared for my times with Deborah.

I just talked about what came to my mind when I sat down in front of her. Most of the time, she listened. The only times she offered her opinions were when I was not sure about myself.

Besides with Dr. F and Deborah, I started talking to my close friends about my experience again. This time, I opened up completely. Luckily, they all listened and didn't shun me. Like old times, we went out to nice restaurants for dinners. I talked about my experience at the hospital, what I learned, and how lucky I felt I was compared to others whose stories were like mine.

I met with my friend Jennifer and asked her to tell me what she remembered from my first breakdown. She remembered some things I did not. She said we had decided to go and watch a movie on a Friday afternoon without telling anyone. My managers had worried for me. One of them called Jennifer and asked where I was. That was out of character for me, skipping work to see a movie. She also said that when we had a dinner together, I was telling her about the voice I was hearing. She didn't know what to do. She ended up telling Chris. She remembered when I called Chris over the weekend, and then she and I had gone to see a doctor on Monday even though I'd just wanted a sleeping pill. She went with me to get my medication, which I did not remember at all. As she was telling me what happened, I felt like I had asked her these questions already. *How many times have I asked her what happened?* I needed to remember what she said once and for all.

I talked to a few more close girlfriends. They told me they were very scared for me right before I went to the hospital. Throughout my experience with schizophrenia, I was happy, hopeful, disappointed, or frustrated, but never scared. I never felt that my life was in danger. But my friends did feel my life was at stake if I did not recover from my symptoms or get the treatment I needed. They felt I would lose the life I had as I knew it. So they had consulted with each other and tried to figure out how they could best help me.

I started to hear of friends of friends and relatives of friends who were dealing with schizophrenia as well. A good friend's cousin had been living with schizophrenia all his life. He needed heavy medication. Even that did not always help. He lived in assisted living. He could not work. His family tried to take care of him. Another woman from work was married to a man who was dealing with schizophrenia. One day, out of rage, he drove his car into a wall. He was hospitalized for a long time. He really could not take care of himself. Since then, they had gotten a divorce. Stories of schizophrenia became more common.

Although I was grateful about being treated well, there were things I had not liked about how I got to my recovery phase. While my friends were trying to be helpful, they did not really know what to do. Some of their actions felt overly chaotic. We all had to learn, and I didn't know less than anyone else. Now I had figured out how I wanted to be helped. I collected the contact information of my current treatment team, which included Dr. F and Deborah, and sent that to my close friends. I outlined different scenarios. If my friends were concerned, they should contact Deborah first. If there was an emergency, they could contact my clinic. Having the right people in place should prevent me from having another breakdown or ending up at an expensive hospital. As much as the hospital had been a very caring place to be, I hoped I'd never go back.

Now that I was not working full-time, I had time to read again. Before McLean, I had never looked into reading about schizophrenia. Now I wanted to continue to learn about other people who had experienced the illness. What happened to them? How did they deal with this condition? What happened to their lives? I started reading memoirs by people suffering from schizophrenia and by their parents, plus guides, self-help books, and the history of psychiatry.

One of the books I read about schizophrenia was told from both the father and the sick son's perspective. I realized that even though I felt perfectly safe while I was in the middle of my truth-finding, my friends very much felt I was in the middle of psychotic episodes. In other words, they felt that something was not right with me and that I might be in danger even though I just wanted to figure out who was talking to me.

The voices I heard were mostly nice. From *Surviving Schizophrenia* by E. Fuller Torrey, I learned that a very small percentage of people experience kind voices. My first voice Joe sounded like a nice young man my age. There had been a couple in my living room talking about what I was doing while I was reading a book. There had been a voice of a close friend who asked me to call her because she had not heard from me in a while. There had been friends playing a word game with me. "Continue this phrase. Everything I do, I do it for ___." When I had been walking to work, another couple of friends talked to me about music. With the exception of being frustrated about not sleeping well, I could spend all day with my voice friends.

I also learned that scientists are not exactly sure how schizophrenia is caused. Our brain is so protected that it's hard to study and observe it. All we know is there are three common factors that can cause schizophrenia: heredity, environment, and brain chemistry. Now I understood my brain was producing excess synapses and sending messages that were not real.

In addition, other people I read about with schizophrenia seemed to act out more socially unacceptable behaviors. One young man wandered to the beach and took off all of his clothes. Another young woman walked out a second-floor window, perched on the balcony, and was ready to jump until her friends pulled her back. Another teenage girl went running into the woods at camp in the middle of the night. I am not sure who was under the influence of voices. No one talked much about what they heard, just how they behaved. I think either we avoid digging into the world of the voices, or it is just hard to remember what the voices have said.

I learned about psychoanalysis from Elyn R. Saks in *The Center Cannot Hold*. She lived with her voices without any medication. Without my medication, Joe's world would probably have completely overtaken my life. Luckily, I had another choice.

From *Is There No Place on Earth for Me* by Susan Sheehan, I learned about someone going in and out of mental hospitals for years. Sylvia Frumkin had her first episode when she was a teenager. I was fortunate I'd had my first breakdown when I was thirty, after I'd already created a life as an adult. After my first breakdown, as much as Dr. Han was inadequate, he did prescribe Zyprexa for me, which silenced the voices right away. For the most part, I continued to live a symptom-free life in my thirties. Some people might remark that going to McLean in my late thirties meant I was getting worse. I didn't feel that I was worse. I was in the hospital because my friends were concerned. My only hospitalization helped me become more aware of the disease. The hospital stay fundamentally changed what I knew about what I have.

From *The Quiet Room* by Lori Schiller, I kept thinking about being put into a quiet room. Schizophrenia never overtook me so much that I needed external help to calm down. During some of my schizophrenic times, I was able to work. When I was in the hospital, I was still myself. I was never restrained to a bed or a room. I kept up with my showers. I ate during meal times. It could have been so much worse.

After reading these stories and more, and comparing them to mine, I could see that my first psychotic episode was a gradual process over three months that eventually pushed me over the edge. The accumulation of confusion and anxiety over time finally broke me. The more I learned the more I realized that everyone's experience with schizophrenia is unique and personal, and how it manifests is beyond anyone's control. The voices would always be a part of me, but I was lucky, and medication meant I could live a largely functional and normal life without having to listen to them.

## BEING STUDIED

Right before I was discharged from McLean, I'd been asked to participate in a clinical study. I'd never done this before and was very intrigued by it. It made me feel I was doing something good by teaching doctors about a set of symptoms I uniquely had. I felt useful.

A gray-haired doctor came to interview me about my schizophrenic experience for about two hours. We sat face-to-face in my room. He asked all kind of questions, and I answered as best as I could. *When was the first time you experienced an episode? How did you feel? What does "living in a glass house" mean?* While I was talking, the doctor took copious notes. I just kept talking. He didn't stop me from going on and on. His expression welcomed it. He took his time and went through his big binder, flipping through each page, asking, and writing.

Another young woman came to me also while I was at the hospital and told me there was a research study for schizophrenia that involved taking MRI scans. I had never been in an MRI.

I again happily agreed to take the test. The young woman who ran the study came to my room to take me to the lab. She told me it was hard to schedule a scan since so many people needed the scan time. I imagined it was also an expensive test. When I got to the lab, she explained what was going to be done. Then I lay in an MRI tube listening to different audio clips for a couple of hours while the machine took pictures of my brain and body.

When I first participated in studies at McLean, I didn't know what these studies were. I didn't think to ask. After I was discharged from the hospital, I decided I wanted to continue to give something back. At this time, I was so overwhelmed and grateful with the care I'd received at McLean. So many people had taken such good care of me. I was fortunate to benefit from modern medicine and science. It would be great if I could do my part to help others. Since I was working part-time now, I could look for more opportunities to participate in more studies.

I got in touch with MGH and Harvard University in addition to McLean and participated in several more research studies. The studies ranged from clinical interviews, logic tests, memory tests (which I was very bad at), simple question-and-answer tests, MRI scans, and EKGs to keeping a social diary every day for a few weeks and open-ended conversational interviews.

I started becoming more comfortable as a research subject. I started asking researchers I met more questions about their methods and reasoning. I met a graduate student at Harvard who had a brother with schizophrenia. She wanted to understand more of the world her brother was in and to know if social interactions would help with schizophrenia. I met another student at MGH who was studying how schizophrenia affects cognitive abilities. I met another graduate student at McLean who wanted to know if looking at brainwave patterns could help detect a psychotic episode.

During my final sessions with each researcher, I asked when they were planning to publish their studies. I wanted to know if there were any breakthroughs in the field of schizophrenia, especially if I was one of the data points. Often the answers I got were something like: "We are collecting the data first, which will take 'x' years. Then we have to analyze the data and look for evidence. That will take some time. After that, we can decide if there are any findings that are significant." I learned it takes a lot of work to make a breakthrough. Many people are working on making lives better for people like me. But it's not easy.

When I talked to my therapist, Deborah, about participating in studies, she asked me, "Why do you want to be a lab subject?" I told her I wanted to do my small part. I explained it was the only thing I could do for others like me. She surprised me by reminding me to focus my time and energy on my own life first. As much as I wanted to contribute, I did have rules. I would participate in any study that observed me or gathered information based on observing my brain, my body, or my actions. However, I would not participate in anything that changed me, like one where I'd be asked to take new medications. I was not that brave, nor was I in need of a new drug to save my life.

Not only did I gain a deep appreciation for McLean, I also met many others outside of McLean who were working on improving the lives of people with schizophrenia. Researchers and doctors were trying to find a way to identify schizophrenia through brain images and waves. During the first three months when I was lost in my thoughts, early prevention might have stopped me from triggering a schizophrenic episode. There are cases of people who only experience one psychotic episode in life. I could have been one of them.

Other researchers focused on improving ways to live with schizophrenia, especially in developing social support. If I had

had someone to talk to, a therapist, during those first three months, perhaps I wouldn't have gotten stuck the way I did and could have avoided my hospital stay.

Sometimes I wondered how different my life could have been if someone had talked to me openly about schizophrenia during the eight years I was seeing Dr. Han. But then I remembered—Chris did try talk to me about it. The conversation had not gone very far. I was not ready to discuss and hear it. It took time for me to be ready to accept I had schizophrenia.

Living in Boston gave me access to great care from MGH, McLean, and the Freedom Trail Clinic. The staff at these facilities helped me merge the real world with the imaginary world and start an authentic healing process. I learned how to stay healthy, be mindful, avoid ruminating, become aware of automatic thinking, and let action precede motivation. I was introduced to professional help, doctors and therapists, who understood and treated mental conditions in ways backed up by knowledge and caring researchers.

Now that I was ready to talk about schizophrenia, my friends and family listened. I continued to write down my thoughts. They read draft after draft that I wrote, revision after revision, as I tried to make sense of it all, now that I had the awareness of my brain disease.

In the end, all these people in my life made it possible for me to live my life the way I am living it now.

## A SIDE-EFFECT

When I mentioned my weight gain to my friends, they would often say, "You are not overweight!" They were right, but I was much heavier than I'd been in my twenties, and if I didn't do anything to manage it, I would keep gaining weight.

It was up to me to see if I could do something about my weight. After taking Zyprexa for more than half a decade, I no longer felt the sensation of hunger. Perhaps my body was getting used to the medication. I also noticed I felt full after eating a meal.

I'd had a scale for a few years and had been paying attention to the trend, whether my weight was going up or down, rather than to a specific number. During the first year, I just recorded my weight. My weight went straight up for a year, ultimately adding about fifteen pounds. Then I took the gap year in Taiwan where I did yoga and writing every day. My weight consistently and slowly went down about twenty pounds. After I moved back to the US, every time I changed my location, my weight went up. During the holidays, my weight went up. Now with a routine, my weight was holding steady.

I felt I was a victim of my medication. If I didn't have to take Zyprexa, I wouldn't even have the weight problem. I could eat whatever I wanted. Then again, some of my friends were also experiencing weight gain after the age of thirty and forty. Life is never that simple or black-and-white. While I learned to control meal portions, ate more vegetables, and stayed active as much as I could during weekends, I also learned to embrace my weight. I threw away most of my size 0s and 2s. I bought new, nice clothes that fit me. I mixed going out for fancy dinners with staying in for simple meals, so the weight evens out over time. I finally learned how to live with my schizophrenic stomach.

# 9

# STILL HARD, RELAPSES

## 2011

One day a few months after I left the hospital, I heard muffled talking as I was getting ready for work. I immediately reentered the world of Joe and schizophrenia. Even though I was now fully aware of my brain disease, unlike earlier episodes before this day, I no longer experienced the imaginary world completely separate from the real one. Now the two worlds were mixed in my mind. I had more common sense. Right away, I stopped taking my medication since it had stopped working. Someone was talking to me again somehow. I went to work, sat down at my desk, opened my laptop, and immediately googled "mind reading." I read the search results, but nothing was helpful. I asked for a sick day, left work, and came home.

The voices started talking again while I sat alone at my dining table in the middle of my apartment. This time the voices were clear. They were new friends from work, and they came from the right side of my living room ceiling. Rebecca said to Tim, "What is happening here?"

Tim responded, "I don't know. Let's look at the situation here."

Rob said, "We need to make sure we ask the right questions."

Tim replied, "Maybe it's Watson." At work, I was learning about IBM Watson and what it was able to do.

Rebecca said, "That's all very good."

It was Memorial Day weekend. I spent three days at home listening to the voices. I didn't remember to eat. I didn't remember I had schizophrenia. But I did start typing down what I heard. I was fascinated by what they were saying. I even started a conversation with myself in my notebook:

Are you taking your pill?

No.

Why?

Because I don't think I need it.

How do you know?

Because I got off it, and I feel fine.

On Monday, I went to work because I wanted to be with people. I knew I should not be alone. When I got to work, I googled, "How do I know if what I hear is real or imaginary?" I didn't find anything helpful. I googled "reading minds." There was a research article that discussed being able to guess one word from the human brain—nothing as elaborate as a sentence or a thought. *Okay, maybe it's not possible.* Then I asked my good friend Jules to go on a walk with me. Jules and I were often inseparable at work. We sat by each other, worked on the same projects, and went to lunch and coffee breaks together. Jules was from New Orleans, and I'd attended her wedding there. I was always comfortable talking to her about what was happening in my life.

"I want to ask you about something. I don't really know how to describe it."

"Sure. I'll try to help if I can," she responded.

"I hear people talking to me. I'm trying to figure out what they're saying."

"Okay. I don't have personal experience with that. I'm not sure how I can help."

"I don't know why it's happening again," I said, feeling lost.

"Well, are you okay?" Jules asked.

"Yes. It makes me feel better to talk about it with someone. What I'm thinking."

"Okay. I'm glad I can help. If you ever want to talk more, I'm here."

That day I got a ride home from Ahmed. When he stopped in front of my building, I said to him, "I'm in a situation, let's just say, where there are three things that are wrong. I can do something that will only fix two things. Would you do it? It doesn't fix everything, so I don't think it's the ultimate solution." In my mind, the three things were hearing voices, being poked at, and being hypersensitive to my surroundings. The solution was taking medication. It fixed most of the problems, but it didn't fix everything because I was hearing talking again. Ahmed said, "Well, if it fixes two things, then you should do it. There is an upside. Why would you not do it?"

"Because it does not fix everything!" I said.

"Do it. Then try to figure out what fixes the third thing. Take it step by step then."

I went to Vara and Scott's for dinner Saturday night. Scott gave me a ride home, and we started talking. At some point, I told him I was not taking my medication that weekend.

"Would you explain to me what's happening? I want to understand," Scott said affectionately.

"I don't know what's happening. I'm trying to understand what's happening," I said, not able to connect my experience with my illness again. I'm hearing from people. It's a conversation about what I care about. It makes sense. I just listen. I am trying to ..." I continued, but halfway through what I was saying, I had trouble understanding my own logic. I was just being reactive.

"Mindy, you can't think your way out of this one! Not everything is about being logical," Scott said urgently.

The realization that I was not able to articulate my thoughts and Scott's comment both silenced me. I thought for a few seconds and was no longer so sure I knew what I was doing. There was something wrong with my logic, my train of thoughts.

Scott tried to convince me to take the right action. "Would you contact your doctor for me? Do that for me! For your friends. Your friends would never steer you wrong. Right?"

"Yes. Okay."

After five days, I contacted Dr. F and told him I was hearing voices again. He increased my dosage of Zyprexa from 2.5 mg to 5 mg. I started taking the new dosage that night, and the next day I was clear of any symptoms.

This was the shortest relapse I'd had. Looking back, I learned three things. First, I could still be confused by what my brain told me. Second, schizophrenia could come at any minute. Finally, I was still vulnerable. When I tried to fall asleep or was just about to wake up, sometimes my dreams were about the past, the world with Joe in it. I would wake up smiling at something I'd heard him say once. When I fully woke up, I felt badly, but there was nothing I could do to control my unconscious mind. All I could do was be brave and let that part of myself be.

I talked to Dr. F about it, and he explained to me it was completely normal to have this kind of experience when waking up or falling asleep. Even people without schizophrenia might experience such disorientation in between sleep and wakefulness. I now accept whatever my brain wants to think about when I drift from consciousness to sleepiness and unconsciousness then back to consciousness.

I don't know if the next time I hear voices, I will google "reading minds." But I do hope I can do the right thing faster in order to overcome schizophrenia's next visit.

# 10

# DATING

## 2012

I accepted schizophrenia as part of who I was, so when I met new people, I had to decide if I wanted to share that part of myself. This was especially true when I started to date again. I started dating late. My first boyfriend and I had kissed under a waterfall when I was a junior in college. Shortly after the first serious relationship ended, I started my second serious relationship with Chris. Both of my boyfriends had been smart, driven, and caring. After graduating from college, Chris and I both moved to Boston to start our adult lives. We spent twenty-four hours a day, seven days a week together, including working our first jobs at the same company. We became great friends with many people at work. Our social circles were exactly the same.

As a young adult, I knew how to be flexible, to spend my time the way Chris wanted. He never forced me to do anything, but he knew what he liked and didn't like. I didn't know what I liked. Regardless, Chris and I had an amazing time together going to movies, restaurants, and nearby small towns in New England. But they were all Chris's ideas.

Looking back at that eight-year relationship, I would say I was too young to take the relationship to the next level and discuss things such as marriage and starting a family. I didn't know yet what I wanted out of life. I didn't know what kind of person I wanted to be. Most importantly, I didn't know to ask myself those questions. Chris made the same observation about me. Soon after we broke up, he complained about me for the first time in a decade. He said, "You don't do anything." With my easy-going attitude, I didn't ever need to think about what I wanted to do. He planned everything.

When I was with Chris and our friends, I would forget to think and provide my opinion. I loved to listen to Chris and my friends talk. It was just how I was. Most of the time, I truly enjoyed what we did. Once in a while, I would ask Chris to do something. "Hey, do you want to go for a walk along the Charles?"

He'd say, "No, I don't like walking."

I'd say, "Okay, never mind." Now I know I love walking around the city on a sunny day. However, at the time, it didn't feel like a big deal not to go for a walk even if I would have really enjoyed it.

After Chris and I broke up, which was also around the time I had my first mental breakdown, I didn't really date again. I didn't miss being in a relationship. I felt that sometimes a person could be lonelier in a relationship with the wrong person than if they were single.

During my early thirties, I was not thinking about falling in love, getting married, or having kids. My parents had cared only about where I went to college so I could get a good job and be financially independent. I didn't know what to do with my desire for companionship when I had that feeling. When I was alone, sometimes I thought about Joe, the first voice. He was the guy I thought about most consistently. I wondered what had happened, wanting a second chance to re-make all the decisions when I'd been hearing from Joe, so I would not freak out, not get sick. During my early thirties, I often stared at the blank page and tried to write down what I went through in order to help myself think.

Unlike my parents, my friends took notice of my singleness. Paige and Vara tried to set me up with single men they knew. I was agreeable and went on these dates, but nothing happened after the blind dates. My mind was not thinking about men.

At some point in my mid-thirties, soon after McLean, my friend Samantha suggested I try online dating. That clicked; it was the right time for me. I thought, *Why not?* I was curious about these new online dating websites. The first time I went on OkCupid, I felt overwhelmed. I was not in the habit of looking at pictures of strange men. I felt so embarrassed that I soon forgot about these websites. I was not ready.

Four years after I was discharged from McLean, I was ready to date. I reactivated my account on OkCupid again and signed up with a few other dating sites so I could get a good idea of how this all worked. My friends were excited and supportive. Some of them offered to take new pictures of me doing silly things like sitting on a swing. Others read my profile and gave comments.

I had to date with schizophrenia in mind. The first guy I met was French. Because I was excited about meeting him, I told him right away I had schizophrenia—during our first dinner. After he heard that, he told me about his psychic friend in France. She would see visions of what was going to happen. He thought she was amazing and maybe that I also had a powerful gift. I didn't know what to say. I never felt I had special powers that could predict the future, but I appreciated his openness toward my condition. It was a very positive conversation, but it was not what I expected.

Another time I met a furniture maker who had gone to Cornell. Again, I shared my schizophrenia with him during our first date. He didn't seem to be taken aback. He asked, "What's it like?" Afterwards, I dominated a good part of the night talking about my schizophrenic experiences. He just listened. If this bothered him, he didn't show it. The next day we went to a beach together. We didn't talk about schizophrenia again. After the second date, however, I overtexted him, and I guessed that was why he stopped responding. I had other problems to figure out besides schizophrenia when it came to meeting someone new.

Because I felt I had no idea what I was doing when it came to dating, I formed a group of close friends to talk about my dates. I told my friends I was talking about schizophrenia on the first date. I wanted to share and be honest about who I was. The more I liked someone, the more I wanted to talk about my disease. I wanted to find out right away if someone had a problem with it. *Why waste everyone's time?*

Everyone disagreed with me.

Friend 1 said, "Your health status is as important and personal as your financial information. Would you talk to a guy about your financials during your first date?" *Okay. Good point.* I would not talk about money with someone when I first met him. But was this the same as money?

Friend 2 said, "Knowing you have schizophrenia is a liability. Do you think someone would be ready to take on that kind of liability during your first date?" Someone might not care about what was going on with me when we had just met. *Too early and too serious.*

Friend 3 said, "This is personal information. You don't have to share it so early. It makes more sense to share this when you're in a relationship." *Right.* I should wait until someone cares about me enough to share this.

Friend 4 said, "There is so much stereotyping about people with schizophrenia that you should let the guy get a chance to know you first. When he knows and cares more about you, then that might be a better time to share more about yourself." *Yes.* I was much more than just the schizophrenic me.

Logically, I understood everyone's advice, but emotionally, I still wanted to be an open book, especially to men whom I liked. I still brought it up pretty early when I was getting to know someone.

I met a person from Maine and started messaging him. We texted for a while and decided we could be friends. One day, while we were texting, I told him about schizophrenia and asked what he thought of it. He said, "Many people in this world are dealing with mental illness. Actually one in five Americans is dealing with mental illness. You should not feel bad about it. It's very common." He told me that he also had dealt with mental illness in his life.

I slowly came around to my friends' thinking. Discussing schizophrenia so early in the dating process did not seem necessary anymore. I no longer felt it needed to be part of the introduction period. Most of the men I met would not be in my life for more than a couple of dates or weeks. There were other more engaging and appropriate conversations to have while meeting someone new.

With all my dating, I have become much more relaxed about discussing schizophrenia. It's just that it's not part of the "first impression" conversation. I want to discuss it when someone has the potential to become part of my life. There is a natural order to sharing personal information, which happens throughout the dating process; schizophrenia comes later now, closer to when I'm ready to discuss other things like living together.

I'm still not sure if I know what I'm doing all of the time. I have been fortunate to meet decent men while I learn how to date again. Unlike when I had a crush on Dan, I own up to my emotions. I accept my likes and dislikes and whether or not I need to talk to them about this major part of my life. I might get butterflies in my stomach, but I don't get anxious.

# 11

# A NEW BEGINNING

## 2013 to 2015

One day, as I sat on the bus going home from work, my life flashed before me. A year after McLean I had left Medullan and started working at another healthcare company in Watertown. I wasn't making friends at work like at Medullan. Socially, I had an OkCupid profile but had not met anyone I liked. The work was steady; the company was good. But I spent about three hours commuting back and forth to work and had less time to spend with my friends. After a few months working at the new company, I took a vacation to Taipei and came back very excited and recharged. Then it was back to work again, day in and day out. On the bus, I questioned myself. *Am I going to live the rest of my life just going between home and work?* I panicked. I didn't want to live the next ten years of my life this way. I needed to make a change.

The next day I went into my manager's office and gave my notice. My manager said to me, "You looked so happy when you came back from your trip. I am not surprised. I am happy for you."

I decided to leave Boston and bought a one-way ticket to Taipei. Taipei was calling me. I wanted to spend more time with my grandmother, the woman who raised me. She was ninety-six. She would not wait for me forever. I knew I wanted to live my life more purposefully and reconnect with my birthplace.

I quit my job and sold my apartment within two months. I took the opportunity to clean up and downsize. I donated bags and bags of clothes to Goodwill. I gave away all of my furniture, dishes, a mirror, art, anything in decent condition to my friends, anyone who wanted them and could make use of them. The most painful things to part with were my books: guidebooks, novels, biographies, memoirs. I brought bags and bags of books to the Boston Library until I exceeded the limit, and they refused to take any more. On a sunny weekend, my dad and stepmother came to pick me up and what was left in boxes and take me to New Jersey.

My friends and I said our goodbyes. They were happy for me, though they could not believe I was uprooting myself in this way. They didn't know how this was going to turn out. They were glad I was going to be with family.

Like my one-way ticket when I came to the US, now I was on my way back to Taipei with no return plans.

I checked in with Dr. F before I left Boston and made sure I had extra medication to cover the next three months. He also wrote a letter to my future doctor about my history and condition. I didn't know if I would ever find another great doctor who would build such a relationship with me. I also did not know what the healthcare system was like in Taiwan. But I didn't worry about this. I didn't research it. Somehow I believed naively that it would all work out.

My cousin Calvin picked me up at the airport. He was the little Calvin I grew up and shared a bed with. We were no longer little. He dropped me off at my grandmother and aunt's home. Everyone was happy to see me! We could not stop talking even though it was late for everyone.

Eventually I settled down with my own routine in Taipei. I woke up naturally around 10:00 am, went to the yoga studio in the downtown area for one or two classes, then went to a cafe to write for the rest of the afternoon. I'd stop at a little eatery on the street and find something simple for dinner. When I got home, I'd chat with my grandmother, uncle, and aunts. That would be my day, every day.

This was the first time I had practiced yoga, and I loved it. I found it peaceful and mindful. The teacher I liked the best was also a chiropractor. He knew the human body well and practiced in a way that avoided injury.

I also had time to focus on my memoir. Up to this point, I had written bits and pieces. Now I started to piece them together, trying to understand what I had really gone through. In my notebook, I drew a timeline that started with the time right before my first breakdown. I listed the things that had been significant to me: body, strangers, voices, friends, computer/TV. I tried to remember what happened when. I drew a line separating what was real (friends, strangers) versus what I'd experienced because of my illness (body, voices). I made many lists dissecting each event multiple ways until I could see it clearly and understand what it meant to me. I wrote honestly. I went through it as many times as I could. It felt as therapeutic as yoga.

Finding a doctor was an immediate need. Through my two aunts, I was able to get a psychiatrist in the best hospital in Taipei, National Taiwan University Hospital.

Aunt Theresa went to the hospital with me, and we waited for my turn. That was when I first met Dr. Liao. He was smiling when he first saw me. My aunt started the conversation since

I had no idea how to communicate my condition in another language. Dr. Liao started calling me "the Miss from America." I gave him the letter from Dr. F. He read it quickly, which impressed me. "You were at a very good hospital. It seems that you received very good care," he said, folding the letter and putting it into his folder. "How are you doing?"

"I'm good."

"Great. You take Zyprexa?"

"Yes."

"Okay, we should continue with that then."

Dr. Liao saw me for about ten minutes and wrote me a prescription. As I walked out of his office, I was shocked at how many people he would be able to see in one morning.

Inside the hospital, there was a pharmacy. My aunt showed me how to pick up my prescription. The medication from the hospital tasted sweet and melted in my mouth like a small piece of candy.

Like Dr. F, Dr. Liao also scheduled regular appointments with me. During one of the visits, I asked if he could lower my dosage. I told him I felt fine. I was not stressed. Seeing how well I was doing, he agreed to lower my prescription of Zyprexa from 5 mg back to 2.5 mg. For two years, I lived a carefree and stress-free family life, not experiencing any symptoms while I was in Taipei.

I told my aunts my stories a few times when they asked. They thought the American life I had was not too good for me. I should have learned to take it easy. It was hard to explain to them what specifically had triggered my first breakdown. It was the isolated mindset I'd had that had led me to a broken brain. In any case, I was grateful to be cared for by them in Taipei.

My aunts must have told my grandmother about my schizophrenia. On Chinese New Year day, we all went to see a woman who could communicate with a goddess. My ninety-six-year-old grandmother was a firm believer in that particular goddess. After we all prayed for a good new year, my grandmother asked the woman, "I want to ask about my granddaughter." She motioned for me to talk to the woman, Aunt Yue-Jiao.

"How are you? What's happening?" Aunt Yue-Jiao asked me directly. I was slightly confused and embarrassed. I wasn't sure how to answer her question.

Then I said, "I hear voices. But I am fine now."

Aunt Yue-Jiao started speaking in a language I didn't understand. Then she turned to my grandmother and said, "She has to decide what she wants. She already knows herself the best."

About a month later, we made another visit to Aunt Yue-Jiao's again to talk to the goddess. My grandmother asked about me again. Aunt Yue-Jiao said more this time. "She has potential," she said, explaining that I had a mind that could communicate with the spirits if I focused my effort. I was special. I could be like her, one of the communicators between two worlds.

After hearing that, I thought back to all of the voices I'd heard from Joe, my friends, and family. *Was someone or something trying to communicate with me? Was that a possibility?* I didn't think too much about it. I thought my brain was broken, but maybe it was just behaving in a way I did not understand yet.

I reconnected with my friends from elementary and middle school. David heard about my experience with schizophrenia and asked if I'd ever considered I was hearing spirits. He said he thought of "hearing voices" differently from how Americans thought of it. "What's it like?" he asked. He thought maybe I was gifted. Maybe what I needed was not a doctor. Maybe I should speak to someone at the temple.

I politely nodded. "Maybe," I said. I thought back to the days when my auditory hallucinations were full on. I could not sleep. I could not do anything but listen. I was not okay without my medication and doctors. I believe in spirits and powers that are bigger than humans, but for now I am and will continue to be happily medicated.

I also learned about cultural differences concerning single women. As a single woman, no matter how old, I should live with my family and not have my own place. In addition, spending time together with family during weekends was encouraged. My American habits of exploring the city on my own and sitting at a cafe with a bunch of strangers were seen as odd by my grandmother. "You are not alone any more. You don't have to sit together with a bunch of people you don't know," she said. "We have coffee at home which you can make if you want." As the youngest person in the house, I had to respect my grandmother's wishes. I also didn't want to upset this person I loved by doing whatever I wanted. In the end, I did live on my own and spend time at cafes. My aunts had to explain to my grandmother that it was "what kids do now."

I also sensed cultural differences in the treatment of men and women. When I least expected it, a decision of some sort would be made by a man instead of a woman without any special reason. For example, in Taiwan, decisions in the family were made by the oldest brother. The younger sister shouldn't give any opinion even if she had the best idea. I had a tough time with this.

I did not try very hard, but I did look for job opportunities in Taiwan. Unfortunately, there were not too many project manager jobs specific to software consulting. The companies seemed very hierarchical. Again, this was not great for a thirty-something single woman.

After spending time with family and friends, practicing yoga, and writing for almost two years, I decided I was too young to live like a retiree. I wanted to go back to being a productive member of society. I wanted a fulfilling career. I realized I was more American than I might have thought. I wanted to live on my own. I wanted to be able to speak my mind and raise my opinion.

As quickly as I'd gone back to Taiwan, I came back to America. This time it was my own choice to come. I know now I have two homes in this world. As soon as I was back in New Jersey, my friends in Boston called me to come visit. I packed my suitcase for a one-week trip and never left. I took turns living in different homes and spending time with my friends' kids. Boston was familiar and comforting. Most important, people I cared about were in the city. I got back in touch with friends and with Dr. F and Deborah. I got my job back at Medullan and settled into a new apartment. I went out on dates and met new people. I was excited to be back and to start a new chapter of my lucky life.

To celebrate the new beginning, I hosted a housewarming party at my place. Samantha, Paige, Zoe, and Vara sat on the floor near the table in the living room. They were chatting about the kids, all eyes on the littlest one in our group to make sure she did not bump into the corner of the table. Ahmed and Paivi stood in the corner near a window and chatted with Jules and Ryan. Between them, they had five very active boys. At the moment, the boys were fascinated by the light switch on the floor. The living room light flashed on and off, on and off, on and off. One of the dads talked them out of doing that. Levina complimented my new place and met Wendy, Andy, and Lani. The older kids were clustered around the sofa, playing video games. Scott sat on the floor, chatting with Paige's husband. I told everyone not to bring anything. But they still did. I was given a jade plant, bamboo, tiny red roses, cacti, and lavender. *It's good to have more life in this place!* I was surrounded by the voices of my caring friends and their kids. I looked around and thought, *I am truly blessed.*

# CONCLUSION

Joe has visited only once since I arrived back to the States. At one time, he had made me feel magical. He knew me inside and out. He read my mind. He knew my every emotion. There were days when he was the first person I woke up to and the last person I fell asleep with. I probably would never meet another person who would be all that to me.

Over time, I learned there was no Joe. He was a fabrication of my brain. Now the only time I still miss him is in my subconscious, when I'm falling asleep, half-awake, or dreaming in my sleep.

# ACKNOWLEDGMENTS

Many people have helped me in finding my voice and putting thoughts on paper.

I want to thank Benjamin Yosua-Davis who worked with me through early drafts while I was still puzzling different pieces of my memory into something readable. I want to thank Elizabeth Brinsfield who ensured that I had a strong voice and purpose and connected the dots, so I could say what I wanted to say more clearly. To Bernard Chen and Margery Hauser, as my first readers and collaborators of writing, thank you for encouraging me when I first started searching for ideas and reasons to write and share. To my early readers, thank you for reading the countless versions of drafts, starting with the first shitty and fragmented draft, and for boosting my confidence to continue my writing journey.

To my family and friends, Dr. Freudenreich and Deborah, and other caregivers, thank you for taking care of and supporting me. Most of all, thank you for being part of my life. Without you, I would not be able to have the life I have and write this memoir.

# ABOUT THE BOOK COVER

The book cover was designed by my good friend Frederikke Tu, a Danish American artist. She drew inspiration from my story and the Swedish artist Hilma of Klint. Frederikke combined the idea of the brain with scientific and mathematical, beautiful and calm images. When I saw her design, the cover immediately resonated with me. Here is how I interpret the cover art: In the middle is my brain. The white sparkles around the brain are synapses that fire in the brain. I have lots of them and sometimes extra ones. The black dot in the yellow circle could be Joe, my first voice and a voice that I thought about often. The yellow circle is everything that happened around Joe. Then the purple circle is everything that happened with voices of my friends and family. All of these experiences light up in my brain. Other experiences are depicted by the black circles. The bottom part is my normal brain, which lets me live and work. My brain is split apart.

# ABOUT THE AUTHOR

Mindy Tsai is an American memoirist. *Becoming Whole* is her debut book. She has schizophrenia and writes from her own personal experiences with the disease. She blogs at her website mindytsai etcetera (mindytsai.com) often focusing passionately on schizophrenia, dating, and writing, and she sometimes includes fiction, such as short stories. Mindy was born in Taipei, Taiwan and moved to New York City when she was a teenager. Her professional background is rooted in mathematics and science. She earned degrees in electrical engineering and engineering management at Cornell University. After college, she has been working for software companies. Currently, she is a program manager for the digital health consultancy Medullan in Somerville, Massachusetts. She lives in Brookline, Massachusetts where she enjoys food, books, walking, and blogging. She has two cats Bilbo and Frodo.

Made in the USA
Las Vegas, NV
11 January 2021